CAMBRIDGE CENTRAL MOSQUE
THE SACRED RE-IMAGINED

in fond memory of David Marks (1952–2017) and
Keith Critchlow (1933–2020)

CAMBRIDGE CENTRAL MOSQUE
THE SACRED RE-IMAGINED   MICHAEL GLOVER

WITH FOREWORDS BY
YUSUF ISLAM AND **OLIVER WAINWRIGHT**

Author's dedication:
For Ruth, my Guardian Angel

First published in 2024 by Lund Humphries

Lund Humphries
Huckletree Shoreditch
Alphabeta Building
18 Finsbury Square
London EC2A 1AH
UK

www.lundhumphries.com

Cambridge Central Mosque: The Sacred Re-imagined © Michael Glover, 2024
All rights reserved

ISBN: 978-1-84822-635-7

A Cataloguing-in-Publication record for this book is available from the British Library

All rights reserved. No part of this publication may be reproduced, stored in a retrieval system or transmitted in any form or by any means, electrical, mechanical or otherwise, without first seeking the permission of the copyright owners and publishers. Every effort has been made to seek permission to reproduce the images in this book. Any omissions are entirely unintentional, and details should be addressed to the publishers.

Michael Glover has asserted his right under the Copyright, Designs and Patent Act, 1988, to be identified as the Author of this Work.

Designed by Peter Dawson, with Ronja Ronning, www.gradedesign.com
Set in Freight Text Pro, Freight Sans Pro and Oswald
Printed in Bosnia and Herzegovina

Front cover image: Cambridge Central Mosque prayer hall, photograph by Morley von Sternberg
Back cover images: (top) the fountain and mosque entrance, photograph by Sir Cam; (middle) mosque atrium on opening day, photograph by Morley von Sternberg; (bottom) prayer hall and atrium threshold, photography by Matthew Wingrove

This book is printed on sustainably sourced FSC paper

CONTENTS

FOREWORD BY YUSUF ISLAM — 6

FOREWORD BY OLIVER WAINWRIGHT — 7

ACKNOWLEDGEMENTS — 8

INTRODUCTION — 12

What is a Mosque? — 16

Julia Barfield and David Marks: Practising the Art of Idealism — 30

Keith Critchlow and the Sacred Art of Geometry — 40

The Trees! The Trees! — 62

Sustainability — 84

Welcome to the Mosque: A Tour into the Heart of the Sacred — 92

One Week in the Life of Cambridge Central Mosque — 180

NOTES — 200

BIBLIOGRAPHY — 203

DESIGN AND CONSTRUCTION TEAM — 204

GLOSSARY OF SOME KEY ISLAMIC TERMS — 206

TIMELINE — 206

IMAGE CREDITS — 207

INDEX — 208

FOREWORD BY YUSUF ISLAM

The story of the Cambridge Mosque is fairly miraculous. That it ever came to be built, was purely by the Supreme Grace of the Almighty, to Whose name the building is dedicated.

Those who lifted the vision from one of dreams, to campaigning, to final plans and then finally bricks and mortar, are all to be congratulated, but none more so than Sheikh Abdul Hakim, known also as Timothy Winter, may God bless him and his family. It was through our many years of friendship and shared love of Islam, that I became connected to this noble project.

Today, as we step into the doors of a stunningly beautiful Mosque, through a wooden forest of trees billowing above the worshippers, creating a heavenly shade over the heads and hearts of daily worshippers, prostrating to the One Lord of the Universe, a feeling of peace and tranquility is undeniably present.

Our hope is that this beautiful mosque becomes a model to provide much-needed space and openness, to promote better understanding between faiths and religions, away from extremism and ignorance, towards cooperation in the great quest for knowledge and unity, that leads us closer to the Face of the Divine.

I would like to thank and acknowledge the generosity of all those who contributed to help this noble project emerge and see the earthly light of day, particularly the offices of the Turkish Diyanet, as well as thousands of generous donors from around the world, without whom this exquisite Mosque would have remained just a blurry sketch of our dreams and hopes.

Peace be with you.

Yusuf Islam (Cat Stevens) is Patron–President of the Cambridge Central Mosque

FOREWORD BY OLIVER WAINWRIGHT

Behind a grove of crab apple trees that beckon you into a quiet garden oasis, away from the bustle of Mill Road, stands a row of trees of an otherworldly kind. They are formed of tightly bundled lengths of wood, which appear to split and splay as they rise. The timbers branch out in sinuous tendrils that wind and weave their way above your head in an undulating lattice, knitting together to form a sheltering canopy that invites you inside.

The Cambridge Central Mosque offers a welcome like no other. The transition from street, to garden, to sheltering glade – from trees of nature to trees of artifice – is one that defines the essence of this tranquil place of worship, a bold arrival to the city that offers a new direction for what a modern British mosque might be.

Throughout the history of Islam, mosques have had no defined type. The mud-brick mosques of Niger have little in common with the domed mosques of Istanbul. The pagoda mosques of China are worlds apart from the courtyard mosques of Central Asia. Here in Cambridge, Marks Barfield Architects have drawn on the local collegiate vernacular, as well as the history of Islamic space, and their own high-tech sensibilities, to conjure a building that feels utterly of its time and place.

Stepping into the lobby, you are transported to another world. The great wooden trees weave their way into a delicate floating filigree, framing circular skylights that wash the patterned marble floor with dappled daylight. Brick walls of yellow ochre gault clay affirm the Cambridgeshire context, inlaid with raised red brick tiles, which spell out the Qur'anic verse, 'Say he is God, the One', in geometric Kufic script. It is a low, protective space, giving you the feeling of being in amongst the branches.

Deeper into the prayer hall, where the column grid shifts in line with the *qibla* axis towards Mecca, the grove of trees take on a majestic scale, as if rising from a low glade to a grand forest of worship. The columns soar upwards and march ever outwards, recalling the hypostyle mosques of Cordoba and Kairouan, or the work of Paolo Portoghesi in the Great Mosque of Rome. More locally, the criss-crossing timbers might call to mind the fiendish cat's cradle of wooden struts that hold up the Mathematical Bridge at Queens' College, while the leaping arches have inescapable echoes of the great vaults of King's College chapel.

It brings the story of this beguiling building in a fitting circle, given that such gothic stone vaults – long synonymous with Christian religious architecture – ultimately owe their origins to the Arab world. At once gothic and Islamic, humble and high-tech, the Cambridge Central Mosque weaves all these threads together into a mesmerising spiritual tapestry of its own.

Oliver Wainwright is the architecture and design critic of the Guardian

ACKNOWLEDGEMENTS

This book would not have come into being without the existence of an entire series of profitable conversations, encounters (some by chance, others engineered) and collaborations, brief or not so brief. The first and the most crucial one happened on a summer's morning about 15 years ago. My wife Ruth and I were sitting in the garden of the house of David Marks and Julia Barfield in Stockwell. The success of the London Eye was by then long established. What would their next really important project be? Julia brought a leaflet out to the table. They had won the competition to create a new mosque, a mosque unlike any other in the United Kingdom – that was their ambition. It was to be sited in the historic city of Cambridge, so it would need to measure up to other great buildings in that city. I began to look through the leaflet. The timber trees in the prayer hall caught my eye, how they seemed to move together so ceremoniously. Julia explained, with some passion (she is always passionate), that above all things else they wanted to avoid creating a pastiche of other mosques, a mosque in the 'cookie-cut Ottoman style', as she put it. She and David wanted their mosque not only to respect the idea of the mosque, but to create a building which would help to define the idea of a British mosque for the 21st century, a building which would serve as the spokesman of an enlightened Islam, a building which would embed itself within, and respond to, the city where it was sited.

As Julia spoke, I thought of two things. I recalled my own hometown of Sheffield, and of how the Methodist Church I had once attended in Fir Vale to the north-east of the city had sold off its Sunday school building in order to create a new mosque. Some years later the church itself became part of that same mosque. These were both repurposed buildings: in no way did they show us what a new British mosque might look like. I was also very much aware of the fact that the new, purpose-built mosque I had recently visited in Sheffield felt embattled, somewhat ill at ease, and perhaps even fearful in its surroundings – the windows had toughened glass, for example – and far too large for the 19th-century terraced streets that it seemed to dominate. Its immensely tall minaret commanded the skyline. Its inside was a blaze of luxury – the prayer hall, with its sapphire blue carpet, beneath a central chandelier – more reminiscent of a hotel than a place of worship. It smacked of off-the-peg luxury, not of restraint or beauty. Did this style of mosque really belong in Sheffield? I had been made welcome as a visitor, but it was evident to me that my visit was rather unusual, and to be remarked upon. What is more, the building was utterly unlike everything else that it was obliged to live amongst. Was it a good thing for it to be so distinctively different?

I was therefore intrigued by what David and Julia were expecting to do. I also knew that I wanted to be a part of it. Even though I had never written a book about a building – poetry and art criticism were my favourite stamping grounds – I had also had passionate feelings about religion and sacred architecture all my

David Marks and
Julia Barfield

Tim Winter (Sheikh Abdul
Hakim Murad)

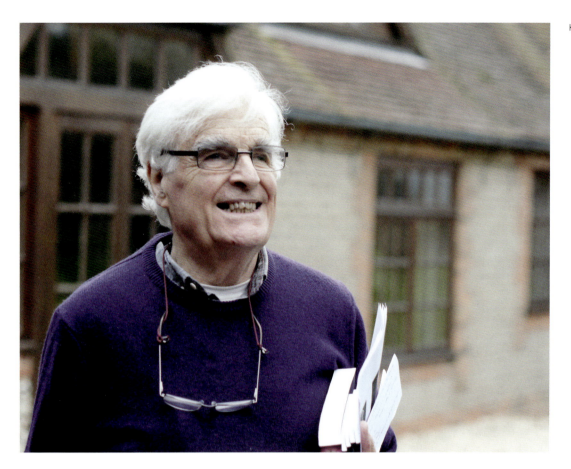

Keith Critchlow

life, and the very fact that my friends had never created a sacred building themselves, and were therefore breaking new ground too, made me feel that I might also find the temerity within myself to play a minor role of some kind in what was happening in the city whose university I had once attended. Later we had many more conversations, planned or off-the-cuff. I sat in on a meeting about the mosque at the Marks Barfield Architects offices with David, Julia, Keith Critchlow, Tim Winter (Sheikh Abdul-Hakim Murad; chair of the mosque's Board of Trustees) and other architects from the practice. I listened as issues of fundamental importance were discussed, from the heft of a door and the design of a door handle to some of the difficulties associated with the practical application of Keith Critchlow's schemes for the sacred patterning of the new building.

A book was mooted, and a publisher with a strong architecture list – Lund Humphries – quickly found because it was soon evident that this mosque would be a project of great significance. Those conversations led to many others with people whose names I shall list now. Every one of these conversations has fed into my story of the creation of Cambridge Central Mosque as I have been privileged to tell it. First of all, I must thank my friend Julia Barfield for our many enlightening conversations, in trains, offices and houses, including hers and mine. Her long partnership with our late and much missed friend David Marks has created a building on which so many awards have been showered, and so deservedly. I have also spoken to several of the Marks Barfield architects who were engaged with the project, some over the entire period of its making, such as Guilherme Ressel, who was responsible for taking Keith's handcrafted drawings of his geometrical schemes and creating many CAD drawings in the course of which that geometry was projected onto the space available, a project that demanded an infinity of patience and skill. I must also thank Gemma Collins, the director at Marks Barfield Architects who also oversaw the technical delivery and construction of the project, and was able to give me an aerial view of the diplomacy required to keep all parties to the project at one. Matthew Wingrove, who was project architect at Marks Barfield as the mosque was nearing its completion, described to me the end-stage issues – from the fitting and the testing of doors, those sacred portals in a building such as this one, to issues of alignment. How does a carpet edge meet the base of a timber tree in the best way to please the eye? The consultant Mark Maidment was brought in at a very early stage to help solve the problem of ensuring that the building, when completed, could lay legitimate claims to being described as the most eco-friendly mosque in Europe. He took me through all issues relating to sustainability. Jephtha Schaffner from Blumer Lehmann came over from Switzerland to explain to me, in great and compelling detail, exactly how the timber trees were made, describing everything from the choice of timber to its shaping, fabrication and, finally, its delivery to Cambridge on trucks, all in numbered sequence. Ian Rudolph, practice director of Marks Barfield who oversees all aspects of practice and project management, provided extraordinary insights into the challenges relating to the funding of the mosque, and described the meetings that took place in Turkey to ensure that the final tranche of money would be in place to enable the

completion of the building. Over at the mosque itself, I have principally to thank Tim Winter, for responding with such eloquence to so many close questions. He is the person whose masterful diplomacy initiated and steered this long project through to a conclusion that has pleased everyone. I must also single out for a special thanks its sole professional gardener, Helen Seal, who spoke so fondly, and with such benevolence, of all the shrubs and plants to which she introduced mc. And, finally, I owe a huge debt of gratitude to Pippa Small, studio manager at Marks Barfield, who has patiently helped me in every conceivable way over many months, from essential photocopying of documents and rooting around for books hidden away in the Marks Barfield library, to providing vital sustenance – tea, coffee, cake – when the pressing need arose, often undeclared.

INTRODUCTION

The official opening ceremony of the Cambridge Central Mosque took place on 5 December 2019. It had been a long time coming. More than a decade separates 2008, the year when Marks Barfield Architects won the competition to construct the building, and the official opening day. And so it has been with this book about the mosque too: there have been stops, starts, and long pauses for further consideration. Unsurprisingly, given the ambition and complexity of the building project, and the number of years that the mosque was under stop-start construction, the issue of money loomed large from first to last. The number of individuals who contributed to the cost of the project exceeds 10,000, and they span the globe. The bulk of the financial burden was borne by public and private organisations in Turkey. Qatar contributed with great generosity. Substantial financial support was also given by the Diyanet Foundation of the United Kingdom. Now, finally, thanks to the commitment and munificence of so many, all those problems are lodged firmly in the past, and the mosque is already a fully mature and thriving spiritual and civic institution which has been added to the list of destinations that any self-respecting visitor to the great and historical city of Cambridge must surely visit. And this book in its praise has been written, too. The praise is much deserved, of course. If any confirmation of that statement were needed, you might look at the list of awards that the building has garnered, which appears in full at the end of this introduction.

As the booklet that accompanied the official opening ceremony reminded us, it is entirely fitting that a mosque of this stature and aesthetic beauty should add to the great buildings of Cambridge, a city associated with the names of Isaac Newton, Charles Darwin, Stephen Hawking, Lisa Jardine, Emma Thompson, Tim Winter and so many others, because it is in this city that some of the most important Muslims have been educated. Think, for example, of the Turkish religious writer and journalist Halil Halid (1869–1931), for example, or of Sir Muhammad Iqbal (1877–1938), the man often described as the spiritual founder of Pakistan, or of Tunku Abdul Rahman (1903–90), founding father of Malaysia. Cambridge also plays host to several important institutions for the academic study of Islam. It is home to the Cambridge Muslim College, the Islamic Manuscript Association and the Centre of Islamic Studies. And what were the special ingredients brought to the project by the late David Marks (1952–2017), Julia Barfield (David's partner in life and work), the late Keith Critchlow (1933–2020) and the Marks Barfield Architects' team? The booklet summarises it very well:

> The winning design . . . seeks to reflect the Cambridge vernacular as well as Islamic themes. The mosque is conceived as an oasis amidst a forest of trees, which rise to recall Gothic vaulting, and meet each other to form a classical Islamic geometrical pattern. The patterned brickwork, which also includes calligraphic texts from the Holy Qur'an, references local Victorian and

View up into the dome showing the pattern by Keith Critchlow

The fountain and mosque
entrance by day

also Central Asian traditions. The entire building seeks to be a harmonious marriage of East and West.[1]

It should also not be forgotten the key role played by Tim Winter (Sheikh Abdul-Hakim Murad) as the client in this respect; being, as he is, the personification of a bridge between the East and West, and the West and Islam.

Cambridge Central Mosque has been the recipient of the following awards:

ROYAL INSTITUTE OF BRITISH ARCHITECTS (RIBA) AWARDS

RIBA Client of the Year 2021
RIBA National Award 2021
RIBA People's Vote 2021
RIBA Stirling Shortlist 2021
RIBA East Award 2021
RIBA East – Building of the Year 2021
RIBA East – Client of the Year 2021
RIBA East – Project Architect of the Year 2021

OTHER AWARDS

Architects' Journal Awards – Best Community and Faith Project 2019

Brick Awards – Brick Development Association – Best Public Building 2019

British Construction Industry Awards – Best Culture and Leisure Project 2019

Civic Trust Awards – National Award 2020

Civic Trust Awards – Special Award for Sustainability 2020

Offsite Awards – Best Use of Timber Technology – Blumer Lehmann 2019

Offsite Awards – Contractor of the Year – Gilbert Ash 2019

Offsite Awards – Installer of the Year – Blumer Lehmann 2019

Royal Town Planning Institute Awards – Planning Excellence Award 2019

Royal Town Planning Institute Awards – Regional Award 2019

Structural Timber Awards – Engineer of the Year – Blumer Lehmann 2019

Structural Timber Awards – Installer of the Year – Blumer Lehmann 2019

Structural Timber Awards – Project of the Year 2019

Structural Timber Awards – Winner of Winners 2019

Wood Awards – Best Education and Public Sector Project 2019

Wood Awards – Structural Award 2019

WHAT IS A MOSQUE?

The idea of a mosque is open to much interpretation. According to Shahed Saleem, author of *The British Mosque: An Architectural and Social History*, a mosque can be a very simple structure, and in fact it need barely be a built structure at all. It is, 'in its most elemental form . . . a wall or an axis marked on the floor (not necessarily even a building), to enable prayer towards the Ka'ba . . . in Mecca', he writes.[1] There is no specific text in the Qur'an which specifies any theological need to create a purpose-built mosque. Whether or not a mosque comes into being depends in part upon the needs of a local community, and the various materials available to that community. In many Muslim traditions, a mosque outside the home is an unknown thing. For those who do regard a built mosque as an essential part of the structure of their faith, it is a site of worship, prostration and self-humbling. A famous *hadith* has this to say, however: 'all the world is a *masjid* (place of worship)'.[2] If it is to be a building at all, there is certainly no requirement for a mosque to have grandiose architectural pretensions. You could even argue that Islam, with its emphasis on the shedding of egotistical impulses, might be less inclined to favour the idea of a building that craves attention in its own right. A building, finally, should not throw up a dazzling barrier between man and his God.

A mosque can be a modest hut, though it most certainly cannot be a former cemetery or a former lavatory, Imam Sejad Mekic of Cambridge Central Mosque explains to me as we talk over tea together in the mosque's cafe one Tuesday,

a little after early afternoon prayers.[3] 'There are no set measurements', he adds. 'It is a place dedicated to worship, which faces towards Mecca, of course, and is clean of physical impurities, without any images of living things, or of objects that resemble living beings. Once it is created, however, God owns it, ownership is renounced to God . . .' That last point is an important one, the relinquishing of ownership to God: the idea of the offering up of a mosque, as it were, to the Divine, a gesture of thanks and homage from the created to the Creator.

When did this mosque-making all begin? At the house of Mohammed, the last Prophet. The very first mosque, as reported by Mohammed's companion Abdullah ibn Umar, was created around a central courtyard in Medina in 622 CE, and it was made of 'adobe, its roof the leaves of date palms, its pillars the trunks of date palms'.[4] A place without embellishment or sophistication, it was used for communal prayer, and it contained living quarters along two of its perimeter walls. In common with Cambridge Central Mosque, which emerged almost 1400 years later, it was therefore, in part at least, made out of wood.

When Marks Barfield Architects began, in 2008, to research the history of mosque-building throughout the world after they had been invited by Bidwells property consultants to participate in an international competition for a new project in Cambridge, they were quite astonished to discover just how various that history had been. So much depended upon regional circumstances defined by geography, the local vernacular, climate and custom, from the variability of materials to habits defined by an indigenous culture. An African mosque would be quite different from an Asian mosque. So little was prescribed by the religion itself. The minaret was not an early feature at all – it had emerged during the Middle Ages. Every mosque had at least one thing in common: a wall – the *qibla* – which was orientated towards Mecca. They also discovered that much of the history of global mosque-making had not been documented at all because a new mosque might be created from the materials of an earlier structure without any reference to that fact at all. So, the global history of mosque-making is a story of accretions, re-creations, adaptations to the needs of human communities. Call it sacred improvisation if you like, with no small measure of Divine steerage perhaps.

And what of Britain? The history of mosque-building in Britain has been a relatively short one. The first mosque was built 135 years ago, in Woking. Many of the earliest mosques were ad hoc affairs, created inside people's homes – an adapted living room, for example. It was not uncommon for a lived-in house to double as a mosque. This is very understandable from a human perspective. A mosque inside a home is also a place of safety and refuge, of course, and many of those Muslims who arrived in the United Kingdom from the 19th century were fleeing persecution. By the end of the 20th century, it was estimated that at least one third of British mosques were converted houses.[5] Many others were repurposed buildings of

various kinds, which might include a school, a chapel, a warehouse or even a cinema. Ever increasing numbers of mosques were needed as the Muslim population grew and grew. The Partition of India in 1947 saw a huge surge in immigration. There was a further surge during the 1960s.

Generally speaking, the newly arrived Muslim population was relatively poor, and in pursuit of work. In Cardiff, seamen from the Yemen built mosques to meet their needs when they settled near the port. The need to improvise was paramount; there was no possibility of state support and the financial means were not available to create buildings of great architectural distinction. There was such a level of informality about the creation of a mosque – a mosque could be almost anything. Beauty was not a primary consideration. Many of these structures were awkward hybrids, assemblages without much sophistication. What is more, there was no requirement to register the existence of a mosque, which makes it very difficult to estimate accurately how many mosques were in existence at any particular historical moment. Or how many exist now. In 1961 there were said to be only seven mosques in the United Kingdom. By 2001 there were 614.[6] Shahed Saleem gave the number in 2018 as approximately 1500, and suggested that about 90 per cent of the mosques in the United Kingdom have been built since 1980.[7]

The first purpose-built mosque in Britain was created in Woking, south-west of London,

The Shah Jahan Mosque, Woking

in 1889 (one of its founding trustees was Sir Thomas Walker Arnold, the great-grandfather of Julia Barfield, one of the two architects of Cambridge Central Mosque). Its address is Oriental Road, and it is indeed a piece of extravagant Victorian Orientalism in the Mughal style, which is powerfully redolent of Rudyard Kipling and the mystically fabled East. Its appearance when we visit it now also reminds us of the uses to which this kind of orientalising was later put, once its style of making had fallen out of favour for a sacred structure: amusement arcades and ballrooms. It has crisply stepped battlements, and a green dome which looks a little deflated at the moment. It sits, beautifully posed, inside its own walled garden, embraced by a canopy of mature trees, and well back from the grinding noise of the road (it has this element of sequestration at least in common with Cambridge Central Mosque).

This was not only the first English mosque, but also the first purpose-built mosque in Europe. The architect was a Christian called William Isaac Chambers, and its founder a polyglot Hungarian Jew called Professor Gottlieb Leitner who later in life converted to Christianity. You can read their stories in well-maintained plaques set into the wall beside the mosque's arched entrance. The building's making was funded by the Sultan Shah Jahan Begum, the female ruler of the princely state of Bhopal. This was Chambers's first attempt at mosque-building. As with David Marks and Julia Barfield, he prepared himself for the challenge by studying and visiting many mosques, principally in India, Egypt and Turkey. The Shah Jahan Mosque is therefore something of an extravagant confection. Nikolaus Pevsner, the great chronicler of the buildings of England, gave it some praise, calling it 'dignified' and much better than many other 'mock oriental buildings'. In fact, it was, he wrote, 'as pretty as Brighton pavilion'.[8] In summer the garden does the mosque proud. There is a fountain not far from

WHAT IS A MOSQUE? 19

its main door, and a scent of roses on the air as you approach. By the 1920s the Shah Jahan Mosque was, alas, out of fashion. It was regarded as too exotic and too fantastical a structure for its own good. Thankfully, a local campaign saved it from destruction during that decade, and now it is regarded as a building of great historical importance.

The orientalist style lived on for decades of course, but its use came to be associated with recreation and frivolity – think of local piers, ballrooms and the amusement arcades so familiar in seaside towns. With the benefit of hindsight, we can now see that the Shah Jahan Mosque is the first surviving indication of what would in time be a radical shift. It represents a legitimatising of the idea of the mosque as a structure which would come to play an increasingly important role in the civic and religious life of the United Kingdom. The mosque was no longer to be a hole-in-the-corner affair. It would move away from the margins towards the centre. And with that would come a new confidence to reflect a certain pride in belonging at last. Cambridge Central Mosque would not only find its historical moment, but also do that moment its justice.

A young imam called Khalil Mohammed, standing at the entrance to the garden of the Shah Jahan Mosque, greets me warmly when I visit.[9] We both watch as a group of schoolchildren file into the building to be taught about how and where Muslims worship. He is so ready to have a conversation because he knows the Cambridge Central Mosque very well – he himself had been a student at Cambridge Muslim College, and he is quick to praise the new mosque for its power to delight and surprise, its spaciousness and its lack of clutter. Unlike so many other mosques, Khalil tells me, it reveals nature as the source of true beauty by using such a range of natural, simple and inexpensive materials – brick and wood. There is so little colour, no use of expensive metal and no pillars. He had never heard of the idea of an eco-friendly mosque before. He marvels at the fact that quotations from the Qur'an are written with the use of bricks. And how the light plays on the woodwork! He talks of how the building seems to insert Islam into modernity. The first British imams, he explains to me, knew too little of the customs of the country to which they were coming. The most important matter is this: the issue of alienation, or rather the lack of it. The Cambridge Central Mosque does not seem to be an excluded place. It belongs in England. 'There is such a sense of tranquillity there', he says. 'The place puts you in a state of such mental preparedness. I caught myself thinking: Islam represents the completion of the Abrahamic tradition . . .' – that tradition includes Christianity, of course. 'There is so much ignorance', Khalil tells me. 'We believe in Jesus too, just as we believe in all the prophets . . .'

There is one other way in which the Shah Jahan Mosque divides itself off, rather starkly, from Cambridge Central Mosque. As you approach the perimeter wall of its delightful garden, it displays a list of 12 prohibitions, many described in some detail, on a green noticeboard attached to a stout metal post, everything that you must not do or even think of doing before you enter the mosque. No speeches without the prior consent of the management, for example. No unaccompanied children under the age of 12. No fly-tipping. And so it goes on. So much of this reads like unnecessarily anxious overkill. That tone – that rather chilling sense of prohibition, the fact that you are likely to be wrong before you are ever right – is completely lacking at Cambridge Central Mosque. Even though it does discourage eating in the prayer hall, would not readily welcome a yapping dog, and expects calm and orderliness, it does not wear its prohibitions on its sleeve as a sort of unwelcome first test for those blunderers who are naturally presumed to be ignorant or unwary. It does not put us off before we even begin. It expects us to be mature and responsible enough to respond to the atmosphere of calm and respectfulness that its very presence seems to induce, and then for us to act accordingly.

Somewhat surprisingly, and by comparison with Cambridge Central Mosque, the interior of the Shah Jahan Mosque is extraordinarily modest in size. Three long strides take us from the door to the *qibla* wall. A chandelier hangs beneath its central dome. Two small bookcases, one on either side of the *mihrab*, offer a small library of Islamic reading matter: a small hardback, for example, describes the 90 names of Allah. Qur'anic inscriptions are everywhere. Green, the colour of Islam, dominates – from the paintwork of the main entrance door, window tracery and the ogival arches, to lampshades

and carpets. Even the Henry vacuum cleaner is green. Three fezes and an assortment of head coverings wait in readiness, bathed in sunlight, on the windowsill. A *mashrabiya* screen is folded back against the wall.

Pevsner's reservations about the Shah Jahan Mosque are question-begging, and they relate directly to the challenge that would be faced by David Marks and Julia Barfield when the time came for them to make their response to the question of how to approach the building of a mosque for our times. That last remark of Pevsner's about Brighton Pavilion troubles. He seems to have regarded the Shah Jahan Mosque as slightly unserious – insofar as he was ready to compare it to the play palace of a regent who had little time for moral rectitude. How to find the right architectural idiom for a new British mosque then, one that would both be recognised as belonging to the 21st century, and represent the enlightened face of Islam? How to create a building that would feel authentic, both of its moment and respectful of the past?

The fact that the Shah Jahan had been built to be a mosque and nothing else was groundbreaking, the first evidence that Islam was to have serious representation in a land without Islamic traditions. As we have seen, the majority of British mosques in the past have been repurposed buildings – a house, a schoolroom, a former Methodist chapel. The mosque on Mawson Road in Cambridge, which opened in 1984, had once been a chapel. Within 20 years of opening its doors as a mosque, it had more than reached its capacity as a place of

The Abu Bakr Islamic Centre, Cambridge, bursting at the seams in 2001

worship. Its Friday lunchtime congregation had grown from around 40 to 700. A photograph shown in the *Cambridge Evening News* in 2001 shows rows of worshippers fully prostrating themselves out in the street, bare feet facing out towards the traffic.[10] What a shocking sight! Where next for that congregation? What building could ever be large enough to accommodate the ever-growing Muslim population of Cambridge? That story would end with the creation of Cambridge Central Mosque, which opened its doors in 2019, and contains a prayer hall of a sufficient size to accommodate 1000 worshippers.

But the history of the recognition of Islam in Cambridge in fact dates from within two years of the opening of the Shah Jahan Mosque. The Cambridge Majlis, the first society to formally recognise the importance not only of the presence of Muslims in Cambridge but Indians of all persuasions, and to bring them together as a community, was created in 1891. Seventy years on, in 1962, Friday congregational prayers began to be held in Pembroke College. Tim Winter, then a recent convert and now chair of Cambridge Central Mosque's Board of Trustees, attended his first festival prayers in Cambridge to mark the end of Ramadan in 1980, along with about 30 others. The number of Muslims in Cambridge is currently estimated to be in excess of 6000, and the number in the United Kingdom is likely to be double what it is today

20 years from now.[11] In 2022, at Cambridge Central Mosque alone, there were approximately 7000 Eid celebrants. The largest group of Muslims in Cambridge by ethnic origin (38 per cent) is of Bangladeshi extraction; other groups include Muslims of Arabic, Turkish, Nigerian and Pakistani origin – in short, a huge diaspora. In addition to Cambridge Central Mosque, at the time of writing the city currently plays host to five smaller mosques and two university prayer rooms.

There were several important matters to be addressed before work on the building of Cambridge Central Mosque could begin. Given that the history of mosque-building in Britain was, as we have seen, a short one, and that there was no local tradition of mosque-building to be guided or influenced by, what should this new mosque look like, and how should it embed itself? How should an important sacred and civic building in the international city of Cambridge, with significant architectural traditions of its own, present itself to the world? What is more, how could an English mosque claim some kinship with the past without nodding in the direction of the kind of 19th-century Gothic to be found at railways stations everywhere, or to a building which would be more recognisably at home in the long aftermath of the Ottoman Empire? How could it both hang on to some notion of sacred tradition, and look vitally alive as a built structure in the present of a city which is home to a great university established as long ago as 1209? How could it avoid being a pastiche or a strange and alien confection? How to combine quality with authenticity?

A large brownfield site – the largest then available in the city – was found for the building in Romsey Town, east Cambridge, some distance away from the city's historic centre. 'This part of Cambridge had originally been a place of light industry', Tim Winter explains.[12] 'There was a sawmill here once. A branch line of the Great Eastern Railway ended here.' In 2008 the western half of that huge brownfield site was acquired by a charity headed by Yusuf Islam, better known to the wider world as the famous singer-songwriter Cat Stevens. In former times the site had played host to a ten-pin bowling alley, a large warehouse for the department store Robert Sayle, and a garage. A lime-works had once been in operation at its eastern edge. There were various issues which needed to be addressed before planning permission would be granted by Cambridge Council. The building should include residential accommodation; it would need to respond to the fact that the area had few green spaces. 'There were competing needs and competing voices to be aware of, at all times', Tim Winter explains,

The local residents' associations had to be consulted, on all matters, both large and small. The East Mill Road Action Group, for example, was opposed to having more student housing in the area. The local residents' most significant concern had to do with the implications for parking.

'It turns out that there are few hard and fast rules for designing a mosque. There is no requirement to have a minaret. There must be a prayer hall, oriented towards Mecca, with a niche or *mihrab* set within or on the wall facing Mecca. There must be service areas for men and women with toilets and areas to perform ablutions.'[13]

DAVID MARKS

The community was especially keen on the idea of a new green open space because there were so few of them in this part of Cambridge. The Council made it clear that it wanted a mixed-use development, which would include residential and community facilities. Another issue had to do with creating infrastructure which would s erve the needs of the town's international demographic. We convinced the planners that the mosque would include a garden that could be used by the public, that it would have some residential accommodation, and that there would be art in it too. Generally speaking, there was very little opposition from local residents.

In 2008 a private competition was held to find the right architect for the project. Marks Barfield Architects was amongst the practices to be recommended because it was at that time working with Yusuf Islam to upgrade the Islamia Primary School in Brent, north London, and also to expand the intake of pupils by creating a new primary school building and prayer hall on the site. A shortfall in match funding meant that the school project did not in fact go ahead, but the Marks Barfield practice had brought itself to the attention of Yusuf Islam himself, and had proved to be more than capable of working within the context of the sacred traditions of Islam.

The brief for the new mosque was quite particular. The winning entry would need to create a sacred building whose design would be based on 'universal principles' – which means, amongst other things, paying close attention to the issue of sacred geometry. It would also need to embed itself in the local community (which would include respecting the look and the scale of the local architectural vernacular), and also to respond to the broader architectural achievements of the historic centre of a city with an astonishing ethnically diverse population of Muslims. So, it should be non-denominational – in no way sectarian in its appeal. Inclusivity was the watchword, to appeal to all, and to give offence to none. It would also need to address the issue of sustainability, providing a building which would have a minimal carbon footprint. What is more, it would need to be a building of status and real presence, lifting the look and the appeal of a part of town which had often in the past looked somewhat fly-blown and in need of a little loving care. Having said that, Romsey Town also had important architectural traditions of its own – the use of pale buff gault brick, often enhanced by red highlights in its rows of 19th-century terracing, for example – which had to be respected and subtly incorporated. This was not a building which could ride roughshod over powerful local feelings or local traditions. Community approval and recognition was of great importance.

The building had to be open and modern, Ian Rudolph, practice director of Marks Barfield Architects, who worked on the mosque project from the start, explains to me at their offices in Clapham.[14] We sit together in the meeting room with its glazed wall so that occupants can

CAMBRIDGE CENTRAL MOSQUE

'We didn't want to create a replica or pastiche of something that existed elsewhere. The opportunity to do something English, British, excited us. Now that there was a significant Muslim community in the UK it was time to work out what it meant to have a British mosque – of the 21st century.'[18]

DAVID MARKS

both see out to the open-plan floor and be seen, overlooked by a photograph of one of the pods of the London Eye. There was no requirement for the proposed mosque to have a minaret or a dome – although it did eventually acquire a modest version of the latter. It would be the first purpose-built mosque in Cambridge. By the date of completion, the construction costs were £23 million, to reflect the development of the brief and design concept that continued after the competition.

What should the mosque actually look like though? The questions crowded in. Was it to be a cookie-cut pastiche of a generalised Ottoman style like so many of the mosques to be seen in the north of England? What might the architectural idiom be for a British mosque in the 21st century? How should a modern, enlightened Islam be presenting itself to the world? Would there be space after all for a reprise of Gothic Revivalism? Or should a version of modernism win out in the end? Above all, the new mosque needed to rise to the challenge posed by Jonathan Glancey in *The Guardian* in 2002: Why are there no great British mosques? Aside from Woking, the others are 'no more than brick boxes, with minarets and domes applied like afterthoughts . . . determinedly glum'.[15]

The shortlisted projects were ingenious and wide-ranging. The judges included many local voices – this was a building which had to be embraced by those it would sit amongst for many years to come. One of those judges was Tim Winter, who would be appointed Chair of the Board of Trustees and was the man whose vision, diplomacy and determination was so essential to the realisation of the project. A Muslim convert, he is a lecturer in Islamic Studies at Cambridge University. Tim's father, John Winter, had himself been a highly respected modernist architect, which gave him considerable architectural understanding and pedigree. 'The shortlist ranged from a space-age design created by a Spanish practice to Khaled Azzam's version of Victorian Mameluke, which would have blended in so well with the architecture of Mill Road', Tim tells me. 'There was such an enormous range of architectural idioms on offer.'[16]

The winning entry by Marks Barfield Architects was modernist in idiom. The word means more than contemporary in look and feel. 'It means', Tim explains, 'that the architect needs to be faithful to the materials and the building techniques that the modern age provides'. The central idea was of a grove of trees, the presence of nature as its unifying symbol. 'Nature is common to everyone', Julia Barfield explains, when we talk about the architects' response to the brief.[17] 'Everyone can revere nature, irrespective of creed or caste. The idea of inclusivity was so important.' As David Marks observed, 'We didn't want to create a replica or pastiche of something that existed elsewhere. The opportunity to do something English, British, excited us. Now that there was a significant Muslim community in the UK it was time to work out what it meant to have a British Mosque – of the 21st century.'[18]

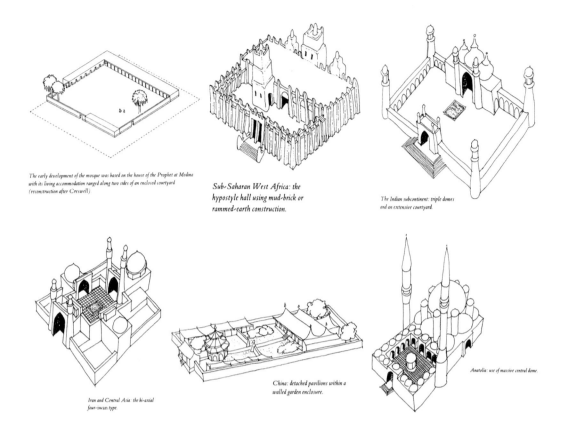

The early development of the mosque was based on the house of the Prophet at Medina with its living accommodation ranged along two sides of an enclosed courtyard (reconstruction after Creswell).

Sub-Saharan West Africa: the hypostyle hall using mud-brick or rammed-earth construction.

The Indian subcontinent: triple domes and an extensive courtyard.

Iran and Central Asia: the bi-axial four-iwan type.

China: detached pavilions within a walled garden enclosure.

Anatolia: use of massive central dome.

(LEFT) Martin Frishman, Mosque topologies and early Medina Mosque, in Martin Frishman and Hasan-Uddin Khan, eds, *The Mosque: History, Architectural Development and Regional Diversity* (Thames & Hudson: London, 1994), after K.A.C. Creswell, *Early Muslim Architecture* (Clarendon Press: Oxford, 1932–40)

(OPPOSITE) King's College Chapel, Cambridge, showing English fan vaulting

David Marks and Julia Barfield researched the history of mosque-building the world over. They observed that for centuries and throughout the world, mosques have adapted to their local conditions – cultural, climatic and constructional – using local building materials and technologies and the local vernacular. They were of their place and time. Various important examples contributed to their evolving thinking, one being the great mosque at Córdoba – the rhythmical flow of its great arches, and how that seemed to continue into the grove of trees beyond its entrance. A public art delivery plan, dated 4 November 2011, refers to the natural world being this point of connection between Gothic and Islam, and talks of a forest of columns that will 'open up to support the roof, which it joins by means of geometrical structures inspired by Islamic design . . .' It will be 'a quiet celebration of the miracle of nature, and the ability of faith to detect mathematical order within it . . .'[19]

A grove of trees would come to be the defining element of the new mosque, and its most talked about feature. Appropriately enough, this grove came to be built in timber, but that was not the material the architects had initially proposed. A masonry structure was their first idea, but timber became the material of choice in the end for a variety of reasons – partly for architectural integrity and buildability, partly cost – but mainly because sustainability was one of the key requirements, as well as the connection with nature. The structural timber columns, or 'trees', are interlaced into an octagonal lattice structure forming a series of light-filled interlinked vaults that support the roof. The vaults engage with the Islamic geometric tradition, using an octagonal pattern – the breath of the compassionate – that is pulled out of a flat plane, rising to the roof from the ground, and all symbolising the connection between the earth and heaven. The trees also recall the English Gothic innovation of fan vaulting which is famously used at King's College Chapel nearby. As David Marks described it, 'Our design for the proposed mosque has emerged from the idea of the mosque as a

CAMBRIDGE CENTRAL MOSQUE

Eşrefoğlu Mosque, Beyşehir, Turkey

calm oasis. The link between the local and the Islamic is expressed though the natural world as a point of connection. We attempt to synthesise the application of geometry, inspired by natural form, within both the English and Islamic traditions.'[20]

The mosque took ten years to build from start to finish. The funds required to build it came in piecemeal, and raising more was always difficult. Funders were large and small, local and international, and schemes to raise money ranged from the modest financial outlay involved in the 'buy a brick' scheme, through donations to cover the costs of such matters as tiling for the walls and carpet for the prayer hall, to large donations from major funders such as Qatar and Turkey. There were pauses, three quite distinct building phases – and even complete stops. 'Every time you pause, prices rise', Ian Rudolph explains. 'It is a high-risk strategy, one that is relatively common in Saudi Arabia and the Middle East, but much less so here. What happens is that you build, say, the shell core, and then potential investors look at it, appraise its progress, and take a view on whether or not the project continues to deserve their financial support.' Important changes were made as the building emerged, bit by bit. Some changes brought about positive financial consequences. 'The foundations, for example, were designed to take the weight of a brick building. Then it was decided that it should be fabricated from timber instead. This meant that the building would be lighter, and there would be a reduction in the cost of the concrete.'[21]

Meetings in Ankara with key Turkish funders generated intense debate around two of the most significant features of the prayer hall, the *mihrab* (prayer niche) facing Mecca, and the *minbar* to its right, the pulpit from which the imam leads Friday prayers. 'Those long and intense conversations all took place around a great, horseshoe-shaped table', Ian Rudolph recalls. 'I had never before witnessed such a level of concentration, nor such a quality of attentiveness, to architectural matters.' A 'table of concerns' was drawn up after that meeting. 'It all came down to an interpretation of old scriptures', Ian tells me. The architects' original designs were subject to modification. The *mihrab* and *minbar* now to be seen at the mosque are much more reminiscent of Ottoman tradition than Keith Critchlow's original drawings – the arch of the *mihrab* is tall and narrow, with 'stalagmite' pendentives. In almost all other respects, the building is entirely faithful to the vision of the architects.

Above all, Shahed Saleem comments, 'Marks Barfield pursued a scholarly approach to historical process, creating a building conceived as an expression of English Muslim architecture'.[22]

JULIA BARFIELD AND DAVID MARKS: PRACTISING THE ART OF IDEALISM

What exactly has defined the work of the Marks Barfield architectural practice? Any definition would certainly include a measure of idealism, a belief that architects exist not only to do some good in the world, but also to share with others an understanding that this planet on which we are fortunate to live is a fragile place of finite resources, and that it must therefore be treated gently, and with a degree of respect. Theirs has always been both a local and a social vision: 1 per cent of the ticket sales from the London Eye, for example, go back to the local community of Lambeth in perpetuity. Such ideals also have much in common with the religion of Islam, which abhors waste, and believes that it is essential for human beings to regard themselves as custodians of the world in which we all must struggle to survive.

Their working partnership began early (David Marks and Julia Barfield were students together at the Architectural Association during the 1970s), as did a vision of what their architectural practice might in time become. On an early trip through South America, they became involved in creating a model for social housing in the *barriadas* of Peru. They had always been community activists, raising half a million pounds to renovate their local park, and helping to rescue the housing terrace in which at first they squatted from near-certain destruction. They also strongly believed that an architect should never be regarded as a stand-alone genius; that great work developed out of a spirit of intensive collaboration; that people needed each other – and needed

each other's opinions. They established an architectural practice of their own in Clapham, south London, in 1989.

One interesting – and perhaps unsurprising – aspect of the work of their maturity is that it is not necessarily easy to recognise a Marks Barfield building. Each project is different from the last. You cannot anticipate what their next move might be and they do not work in series. They have no definable house style. They are not high-end purveyors of luxurious examples of six-star hotels, or of houses, with acres surrounding, in the Home Counties. Their structures are not self-conscious models of ostentation. They do not so much impose themselves on a locality as insert themselves into it, with a degree of modesty. They are aware of the need for buildings to be efficient, aesthetically pleasing and well grounded in their respective environments. Art would always be at the core of any design. Sites can be very sensitive places, in need of solutions which are specific to their place and combine tact and respect.

Think, for example, of the Treetop Walkway in Kew Gardens, which opened in 2008. The near-sky-high structure weaves its way amongst the trees, often within touching distance of the natural world it is meandering through, offering unique vistas, and very mindful of what must be avoided. 'We have always tried to stay free of preconceptions. Each project is different from the last', Julia Barfield explains to me. She speaks with great zest, as if every project has its unique excitements in store.

Treetop Walkway, Royal
Botanic Gardens, Kew,
Richmond

Exploded three-dimensional CAD image of a London Eye capsule

13 (OVERLEAF)
London Eye

We do believe – David and I always believed, and I shall continue to believe – that good design and good architecture are powerful tools for good, both social and environmental. At its best it improves the quality of people's lives and lifts their spirits while drawing on a minimum of the earth's limited resources . . . Each one of our buildings strives to be a unique response to the site and its context. We regard ourselves as creative problem-solvers.[1]

Marks Barfield Architects have always worked directly with engineers and even specialist subcontractors from very early on in any given project so that making and designing go hand in hand from the very start. Their vision is informed by four key matters: mathematics, geometry, nature and science. Three words perhaps best summarise their goals as an architectural practice: beauty, sufficiency and circularity.

So, what exactly have they been engaged in over the last 30 years?[2] Some of their projects could not be better known – the London Eye, for example, loosely based on what everyone remembers as the rickety fairground Ferris wheel of old, but wholly reimagined and refashioned as a huge and stable structure. Its presence, when it was raised up between the Thames and County Hall, once the seat of London's government, seemed to be the very embodiment of the new millennium, and it opened to a blaze of festive fireworks just in time for the year 2000. Marks Barfield Architects bridged the gap between engineering and architecture and challenged the traditional roles of architect and client, as they took on both and became the London Eye's creative entrepreneurs. Its best and most innovative feature is its pod, into which the visitor steps, rather trepidatiously it has to be said (the wheel is always in movement, albeit slowly), for that circular journey. Who would have guessed that you could enjoy

JULIA BARFIELD AND DAVID MARKS: PRACTISING THE ART OF IDEALISM

Brighton i360

36 CAMBRIDGE CENTRAL MOSQUE

emerging 360-degree vistas of London from a giant, glazed, softly enclosing capsule, which would feel not only safe and secure, but also utterly smooth and unbuffeted by any wind in its continuous journeyings? Those pods, built by a French company called Poma (known for its ability to create ski-lifts, cable-cars and snow machines for use in the Alps), provide a stable, safely sealed environment within which to view London at a speed which is almost imperceptible in its gentleness. More recently, the practice has set a vertical pier in motion in Brighton, known as the i360, which rises up and up on a giddyingly long pole.

There are many other projects too, less well known by the wider public perhaps, but public ostentatiousness is a matter of little importance to the practice. Marks Barfield Architects created a community-initiated art gallery in Woking and a new kind of primary school with very special sightlines in Cambridge. The University of Cambridge Primary School of 2015 is all about openness, shared access and permeability. With buildings that form a pleasing circle around a green central courtyard, it offers classrooms without doors, a shared 'learning street' and a covered outdoor learning space. As with Cambridge Central Mosque, there is a great deal of natural light and very low energy use. Science and nature have played their parts in the shell-like Spiral Cafe in Birmingham. This is a building conceived as a sculpture to be inhabited, prompted into being by the graceful spiral of the Fibonacci sequence. The direction in which a building faces is always of great

importance – a built structure should not turn its back on the community it is there to serve – and their Abbey Wood transport interchange in north London pulls together two parts of a divided community.

The Cambridge Central Mosque was a first for Marks Barfield Architects. They had never before risen to the challenge of trying to create a sacred building, but the mosque, when it finally emerged after over a decade of planning and making, was a boldly imagined thing. In fact, you could think of it as the culmination of their work as a practice over the almost 30 years of its existence, part of a continuum of their thinking. Its brief, which was not only to respect and pay attention to universal values, but also to create a building which would have a barely visible carbon footprint, threw up so many different kinds of challenges, Julia Barfield tells me. 'The Muslim population of Cambridge is so broad-based: up to 60 or 70 different nationalities and cultural groups are represented. We had to satisfy them all.'[3] The project, from the start, was a collaborative endeavour, as all good architecture must surely be, profiting from the talents of 25 members of the Marks Barfield team alongside numerous engineers and other specialist consultants. It required not only an extraordinary breadth and depth of vision, but also bold and decisive risk-taking. Several Marks Barfield projects have been created off-site: the London Eye and the Treetop Walkway, for example, and the same approach was taken for the trees of Cambridge Central Mosque.

(LEFT) University of Cambridge Primary School

(OPPOSITE) The Lantern atrium, 75 Hampstead Road, London

We have always worked collaboratively with specialist subcontractors, developing innovative designs with the people who are the makers. On the London Eye we established relationships with Hollandia (who built the structure) and Poma (who built the capsules). These relationships have lasted more than 25 years – later we went on to collaborate with them on the i360 in Brighton. We worked with Britland steel on the Kew Treetop Walkway, and with Blumer Lehmann on the Cambridge Mosque – I regard these companies as the master craftsmen of our time.

The mosque is highly innovative too, as much in what it excluded as included. 'We knew that the minaret as a place from which to make the call to prayer did not exist in the seventh century. It was a medieval invention. Why even create one in the 21st century when an app can do the job just as well, you might well ask yourself?' There is a dome, which was a late addition, and is of course a traditional feature of a mosque, but its position is not overly emphatic. It does not announce itself to the world as an essential or defining feature. In fact, is it not the dome's very reticence which seems to define it? Julia agrees. 'Yes, it is set back and relatively small, and located adjacent to the *qibla* wall and *mihrab*.'

Julia's remarks spiral back around in the end to the importance of the local, communitarian spirit of the mosque:

Even though the conceptual starting point for the building was the idea of a garden of paradise within a grove of trees (the idea that nature is an oasis that lifts us in the direction of some ultimate state of tranquillity and calm), we were always aware that it was just as important to respond to local cultural needs and the expectations of the local community, with its own traditions of making, and its own materials – as mosques always have done.

38 CAMBRIDGE CENTRAL MOSQUE

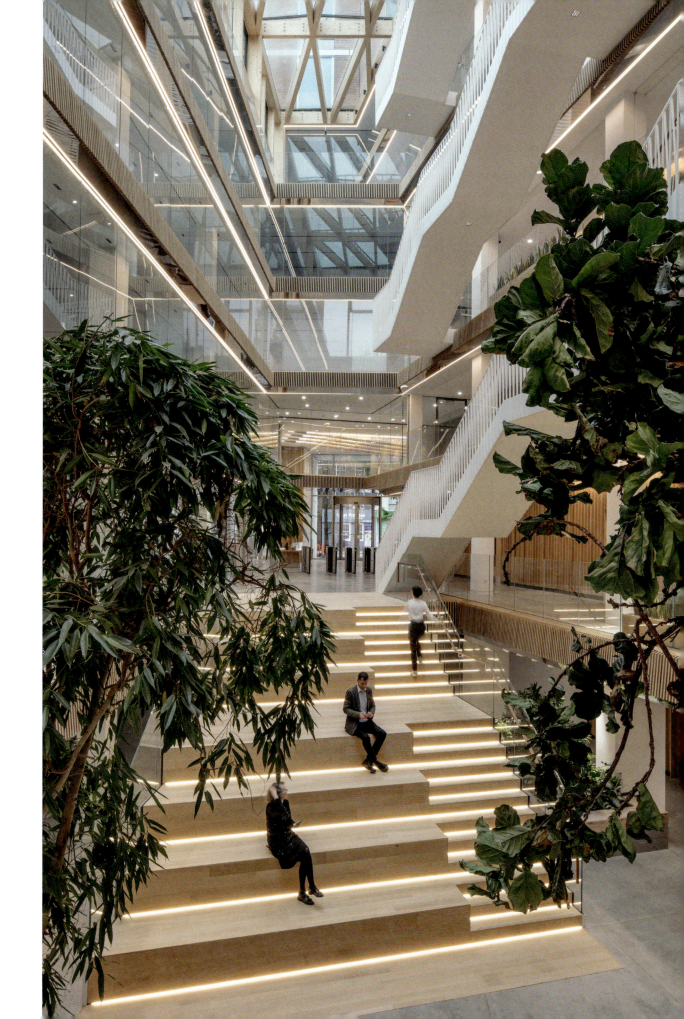

KEITH CRITCHLOW AND THE SACRED ART OF GEOMETRY

David and Julia were tutored at the Architectural Association in the 1970s by Keith Critchlow, who, in the words of Buckminster Fuller, had 'one of the century's rare conceptual minds'.[1] By 2008 he was among other things an expert in sacred architecture and Islamic geometry. He was invited to join the team during the competition stage to create and advise on primary Islamic geometric design work, and Islamic design in general. There was another reason for his involvement. Cambridge City planning department had a requirement for public art to be part of any major projects.

Where and how to begin? What are the fundamentals? At the outset of the project, Keith Critchlow set his ideas down on paper, to remind himself of what any new mosque should be doing, and what its role should be:

A   The primary function of a mosque is a place of gathering to remember God (*Dhikr*)

B   Secondary function is to uphold the Muslim culture and way of life peacefully, to give access to treasures of Muslim philosophy, art, music, literature, poetry.

C   Tertiary function is to support the local Muslim community and enhance intercultural relationships and understanding. It is also a social gathering place.

D   Physical function is to display the most intelligent use of materials within the 'green' ethos, whilst also displaying economy of structure and beauty of expression.[2]

*

Plato called geometry 'the art of the ever true'.[3] Islam concurred – and then proceeded to take what it regarded as a sacred science to ever higher levels of complexity and sophistication. According to Islam, the science of mathematics itself is of Divine origin, a gift from God, and the science of numbers is at the root of all the sciences. Geometry is that which underpins and unifies. It is a form of spiritual bonding. And few people have written more cogently, more fully or more subtly on the subject of geometry as a sacred art than the late Keith Critchlow. In 1984 Keith founded the Visual Islamic and Traditional Arts Programme at the Royal College of Art, the very first Islamic art department within the Western academic tradition, and then went on to teach that programme at the Prince's Foundation School of Traditional Arts.

In 2008, a year before Keith's note was written, David Marks had also committed to paper an early description of how the practice's understanding of the meaning of sacred architecture would inform their approach to the creation of the building. 'Sacred architecture', he wrote,

is there to communicate universal principles and truths. A proper understanding of its symbolic meaning

Keith Critchlow examining Islamic geometry

needs to be combined with the practical skill to embody it in built form in order to see the beauty that shines through the world. All this requires contemplative intelligence, artistic skill, knowledge of the traditional framework, and an ego that does not impose itself upon the process.[4]

Originality would be a guiding principle throughout – but originality, as far as this building was concerned, would mean 'referring to the origin' rather than taking its cue from the modish or the passing. All the geometric patterns Keith drew were original to himself. They were not copied from existing designs. In this way the tradition of geometric art is kept alive.

Keith Critchlow was appointed the mosque's sacred geometer in 2008, at the very conception of the project, and he would work closely with David Marks, Julia Barfield and other members of the Marks Barfield practice throughout (most notably Guilherme Ressel, who transferred Keith's two-dimensional hand drawings to the computer screen, and realised them as three-dimensional virtual objects). Why did this building require a sacred geometer? In a handwritten note from 2017, Keith describes how Sinan (d.1588), civil engineer, leader of the guild of architects in the Ottoman Empire and creator of 400 identifiable buildings, worked directly with three sultans: Suleiman the Magnificent, Selim III and Murad III. 'What we can correctly assume', Keith writes, 'is that any potential architect had to be a master of geometry'.[5] Such is geometry's importance to Islam.

What exactly does a sacred geometer do? The fundamental matter to be aware of is that the sacred art of Islam is expressed through geometric patterning, arabesque and calligraphy. It is the geometer's task, through a scheme of highly sophisticated visual patterning, to give unity to every surface of a sacred space such as Cambridge Central Mosque, from its walls to its doors, from its ventilation grilles to its floors, and, most of all, to point up the cosmic significance of geometry. The cultural value of

Keith Critchlow's concept hand sketch for the truncated cuboctahedron geometry on the Cambridge Mosque dome

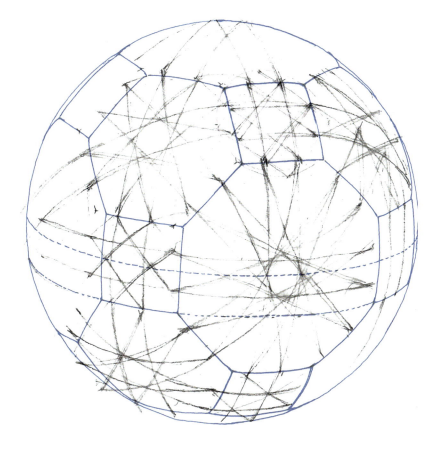

In geometry, the Breath of the Compassionate, *Nafas al Rahman*, is an eight-pointed star pattern with static and dynamic squares overlapping each other. The idea that the divine breath created the basic elements (air, water, fire and earth) is the inspiration for the shape's name. It is a design used in many cultures and regions; its symmetry and balance symbolise harmony and unity.

KEITH CRITCHLOW AND THE SACRED ART OF GEOMETRY

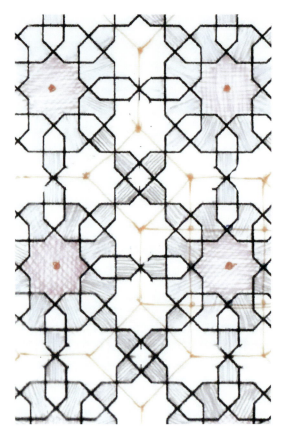

The 'breath of the compassionate' sketch patterning carried through into the Cambridge Mosque atrium stone floor

a mosque, Keith wrote in a note of July 2009, is that it should

> embody the building wisdom of the ages, and express significant unifying forms. These will inevitably express the Unity of Being and the intrinsic meaning of the universe and the unified creation. The rich heritage of Islamic Arts would be expected to be found here: philosophy, poetry, literature, music, all the visual arts – founded on Geometry, which was called by Plato 'the art of the ever true'.[6]

And, according to Keith, what was the primary function of the mosque? In July 2009 he wrote his answer to that in the note with which this chapter opens: 'a place of gathering to remember God'.

Geometry is not an abstract art – in the current sense of the word – because the universe is alive with God's signs. Patterning itself is a kind of spiritual aid towards achieving wholeness. There are celestial archetypes apparent to the student of sacred mathematics which are manifested both in the cosmos and within the very soul of man. Islamic patterns have metaphysical significance. Figures familiar to so many – the circle, the square, the triangle, the hexagon (which often all work together in the form of a repeating grid) – have a very particular meaning to the sacred geometer. Such thinking encompasses cosmology, which is nothing other than 'the logic or study of the laws and intelligences inherent in this ordered universe'. The square, for example, represents the earth or material things, the triangle human consciousness and the principle of harmony. The circle symbolises plenitude, simplicity and cosmic unity. 'This pattern of triangles, squares and a central hexagon is a reminder of the archetypal importance of the integration of the three shapes within one another, as the expression of unification', Keith wrote in *Islamic Patterns*.[7]

The underlying geometry that Keith developed for the mosque was a repeating

44 CAMBRIDGE CENTRAL MOSQUE

octagonal pattern with a star at its centre based on the idea of 'the breath of the compassionate', and this pattern would serve as a geometric anchor for all aspects of the decoration within the building. The patterning of a mosque, as Shahed Saleem explains in *The British Mosque*, needs to possess the flexibility of infinite extendibility. 'Each pattern can expand and contract and can be symmetrically reproduced . . . each part of the design answers every other part and is capable of extension to infinity . . . as a metaphor of eternity.'[8] As David Marks himself once wrote:

> Artists evoke symbols that connect us to our deeper selves, they can help us along the journey of our own lives. Religious art recognises that. The artist puts the objects of this world together in such a way that through them you will experience that light. That radiance which is the light of our consciousness and which all things both hide and, when properly looked upon, reveal.[9]

Keith was very much a hands-on sacred geometer, but he was not one who would necessarily explain the evolution of his decorative scheme as it developed. I ask Julia Barfield, did he ever write down what the phrase 'the breath of the compassionate' actually meant? Or how the idea would manifest itself across the mosque? No. She had asked him several times, but he never did. How to unlock this mystery then? Gemma Collins recalls that he would sit next to her in the office, scrutinising her every move. His dislike of machines extended to a suspicion of drawing on the computer, the fact that it seemed to be several steps away from the human touch, to be handing over responsibility to an unfeeling, impersonal force. There is a paradox here though. His own drawings were all in pencil, which means that, though unique, they were also imperfect in a way that a computer's could not be. The huge challenge, always, was to take those two-dimensional hand drawings, and to extrapolate them into three-dimensional forms.

Ian Rudolph, practice director at Marks Barfield Architects, recalls Keith explaining the meaning of 'the breath of the compassionate' in the following way: 'When you look up at the stars, what you are seeing is the very last gasp of air captured. The breathing out of those stars creates a geometry . . .'[10] It is a metaphysical world view in all its ungainsayable purity.

Tim Winter explains the religious significance of the idea:

> It is a theological phrase which refers to God's creation of the world: everything is 'exhaled' by Him, out of his love and compassion for things that had previously not enjoyed the blessings of existence. It is also an idiom which refers to the mystery of life. Nature is a particular indicator of Divine agency. We feel at home when we are surrounded by it. It is about the preservation and the celebration of life. Trees include us in nature, they enfold us.

THE KAIROS PERSPECTIVE
© K.B.C. for Kairos

THE VARIATIONS ON THE BREATH of the COMPASSIONATE Pattern.

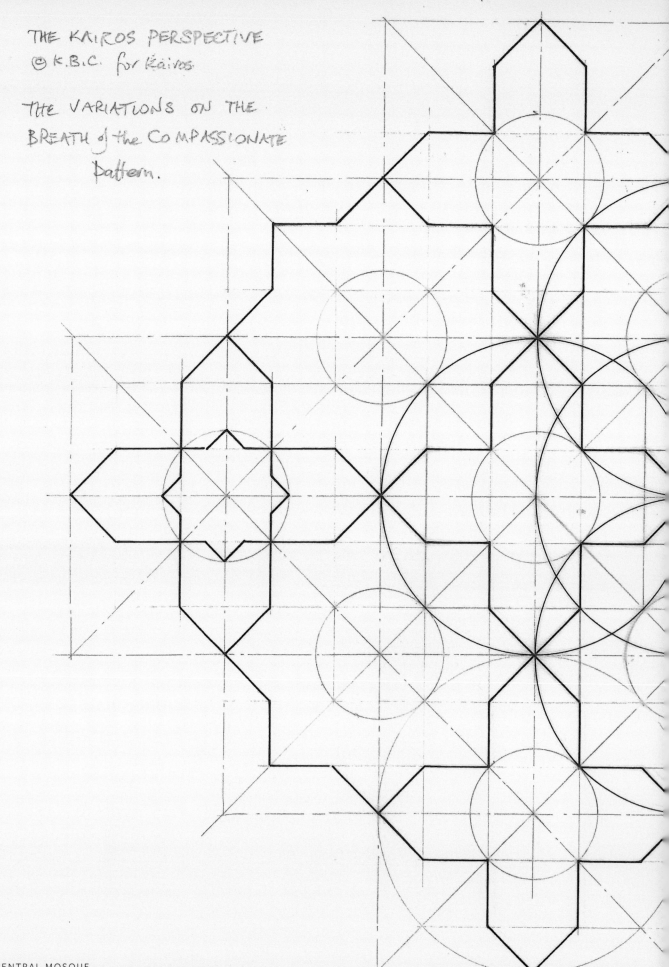

CAMBRIDGE CENTRAL MOSQUE

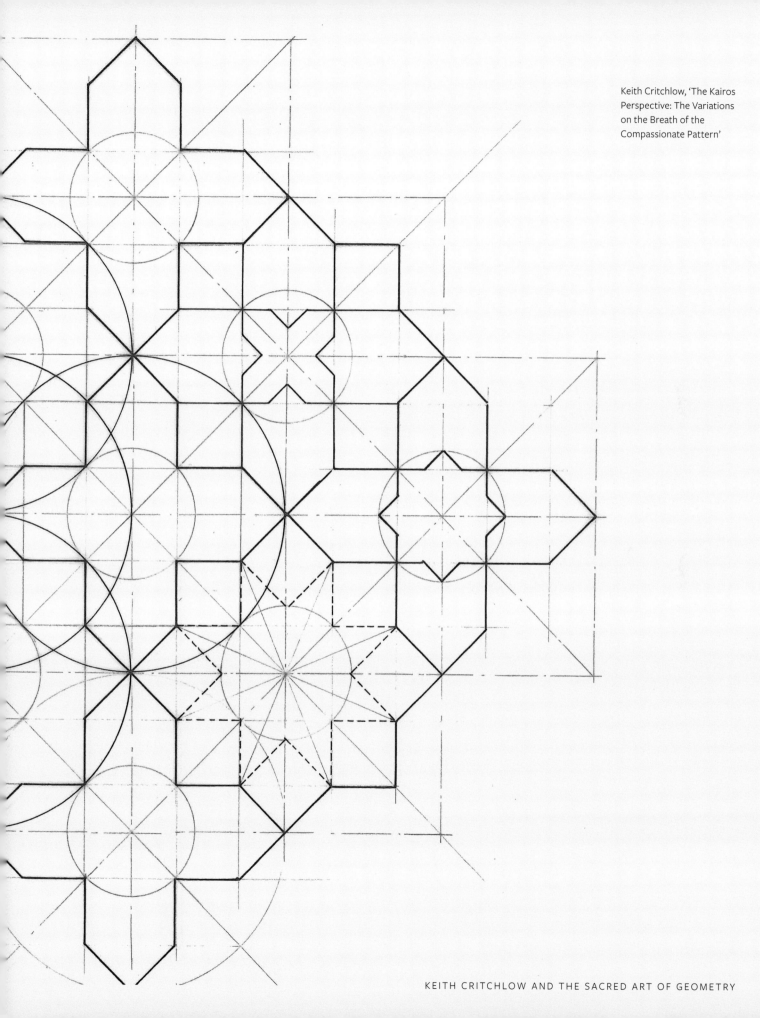

Keith Critchlow, 'The Kairos Perspective: The Variations on the Breath of the Compassionate Pattern'

(BELOW) Geometrical interpretive breakdown of 'the breath of the compassionate' by Marks Barfield Architects

We reactivate our presence as God's agents. Art exists to remind us of what is just below the surface – geometry and symmetry, those physical constants, offer proof of the existence of order, a calm reminder that the world is orderly, and under control. Otherwise, there would be pure anarchy.[11]

On a more basic level, and having stared hard at the way in which the appearance of the convex seems to relate to the concave throughout the Cambridge Central Mosque, you could also say that this enigmatic turn of phrase refers to the way in which a human being establishes a regular rhythm of breathing, in and out, lifelong, from the concave to the convex and back again.

Keith's proposed geometry begins with a square superimposed upon another square, with a star at its centre. The second square is then swivelled by 90 degrees in order to create an octagon. The scheme becomes ever more complex as it grows, and lines flow, interweave and intermesh, and it had to be accommodated within a space of very particular proportions. The drawings, created by the human hand with the aid of nothing but a pair of compasses, were then subjected to manipulation by the computer, and fabricated anew as they were contracted, extended, thinned or thickened. Hand drawings became virtual drawings, which were then subject to endless manipulation on-screen.

The flavour and intricacy of Keith's thinking is captured very well in yet another handwritten

Form

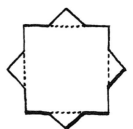

Expansion

Contraction

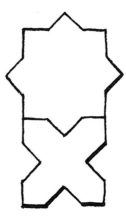

The Breath of the Compassionate

48 CAMBRIDGE CENTRAL MOSQUE

The prayer hall design at competition stage: the structure was at this time envisioned with masonry fan vaulting.

note, also of 2009, which describes his approach to the development of the geometry of the original *minbar* (which, in the end, was rejected in favour of an Ottoman solution). So much is influenced by precedence, ancient ways of doing things revitalised for the present. Keith begins by justifying his solution with reference to the practice of Sinan, his illustrious predecessor:

> The great Ottoman architect Sinan himself designed this piece of geometry. It is the profound integration of a series of normally incompatible symmetries that is four fold, five fold, six fold, seven fold and eight fold. We have introduced two more for this special occasion of sixteen fold and twelve fold by doubling the eight and six in two central places . . .[12]

Guilherme Ressel was the man most often at the keyboard, integrating two-dimensional geometric patterns and artwork from Keith into the architectural three-dimensional design.

'The digital fabrication of the space on the computer was very much about the realisation of the architect's vision', he explains. In fact, several visions came together in one: the architectural fan-vaulting array of trees came from David and Julia, the rigidity of 'the breath of the compassionate' pattern from Keith. The structural elasticity of the geometry of laminated timber (with a minimum radius of 1.5 m) was Blumer Lehmann's crucial contribution. 'At all times we had to be mindful of the function and use of the building by its worshippers. Every one of these constraints or guidelines was considered when developing the overall timber structure, and many iterations were proposed and tested out before we were able to satisfactorily combine these various visions.'[13]

The idea of the fan vaulting had also emerged through visits David and Julia made to King's College Chapel in Cambridge, the mosque in Parioli, Rome, Westminster Abbey's Chapter House and the mosque at Córdoba. 'The need for respectfulness encompassed not only the idea of geometry', Guilherme comments,

KEITH CRITCHLOW AND THE SACRED ART OF GEOMETRY

(**OPPOSITE**) Many options for the tree geometry were tested. The roof lights were originally located between the trees and were eventually moved to above them.

but also the sacredness of the number four, being mindful, always, of the proportions of the space to be occupied, and the demands of the overall structure, placing the octagons in relation to each other, shifting the position of the skylights in relation to the tops of the trees, always changing the sizes as we thought and thought again about the space that was available. It was like putting a giant puzzle together.

Fundamental changes happened quite early on:

We won the competition in 2008 with the understanding that the structure of the building would be masonry, but by 2009 it had become clear to us that this would not work as a solution because hidden structural support would be needed. What was seen would be 'dressing' only. It would not be what it was seen to be. It would lack authenticity. And so, in 2009, timber became the material of choice. From then on the challenge would be how to work with bent timber in order to realise this vision of a grove of trees . . .

Once it had been decided that the grid of trees would become the basic structure of the mosque, they had to think about the positioning of the roof lights, and where they should sit. The issue of sustainability was crucial to this stage of the thinking. 'The roof lights went from being between the trees to above the trees. So much changed and changed

again before any final solution could be arrived at. Only the *mashrabiya* screen did not change.' As Guilherme speaks, he calls some of the forms back into being on screen, shifting them backwards and forwards, elongating, spinning, twisting, turning concave into convex and then back again, and all at a touch of the keyboard. Everything looks so open to question and subject to near ceaseless, on-screen experimentation – as was indeed the case. The choices looked almost bewilderingly infinite.

We were riffing on three basic geometrical elements in order to achieve the art of the possible. The computer too is an extension of the human brain. It is not an impersonal tool. In fact, it can even go beyond what the hand can achieve. What height could we go to? We were probing the limits of the possible. There were always so many different options to be explored. We contracted and inflated the octagons, over and over. Keith drew with the hand to please the eye in two dimensions, but the rigours of the computer were something slightly different, taking 2-D into 3-D poses separate challenges and offers alternative solutions. It was a series of iterative processes. There was such an interweaving and an intermeshing of forms.

Everything was in contention – including the patterning of the brick tiles that would cover the inner walls of the atrium and clad the outside of the building:

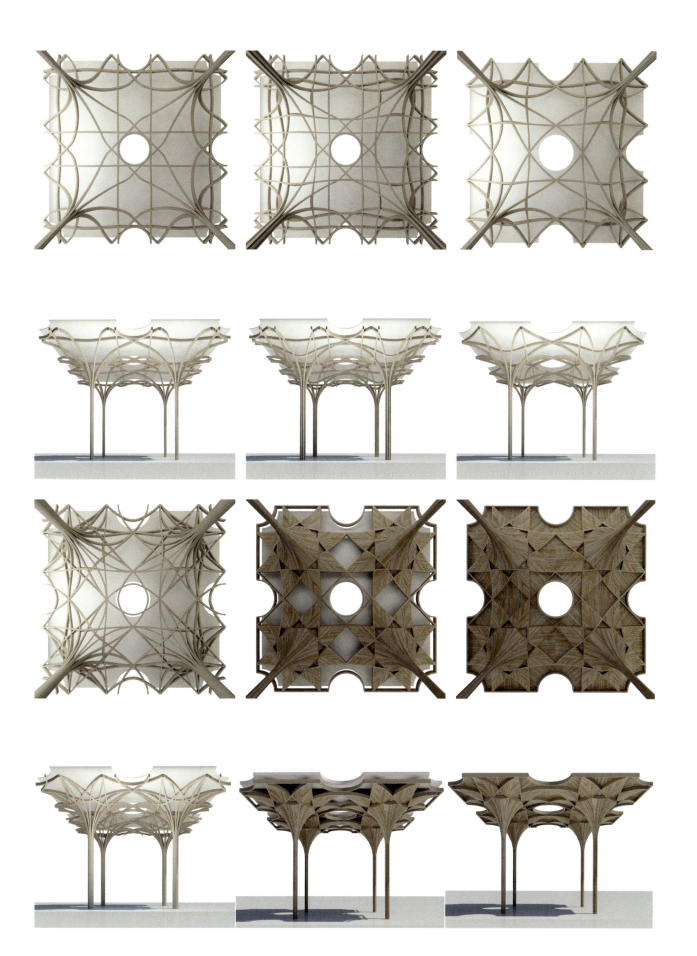

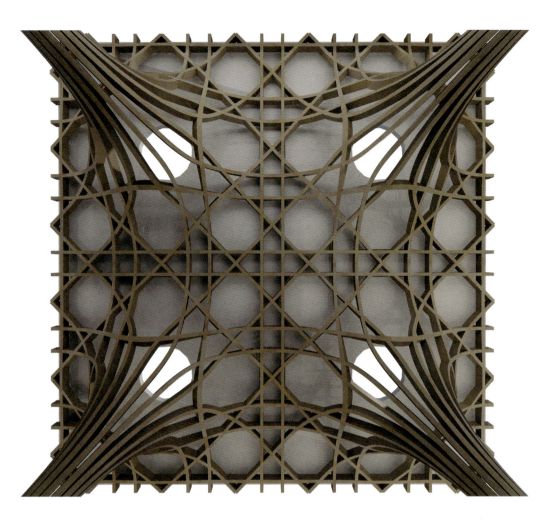

(LEFT) Current tree set, ceiling view

(BELOW) Current tree set, front view

(OPPOSITE TOP) Early geometric study of the masonry fan vaulting at competition stage

(OPPOSITE BELOW) The trees, structural model

52 CAMBRIDGE CENTRAL MOSQUE

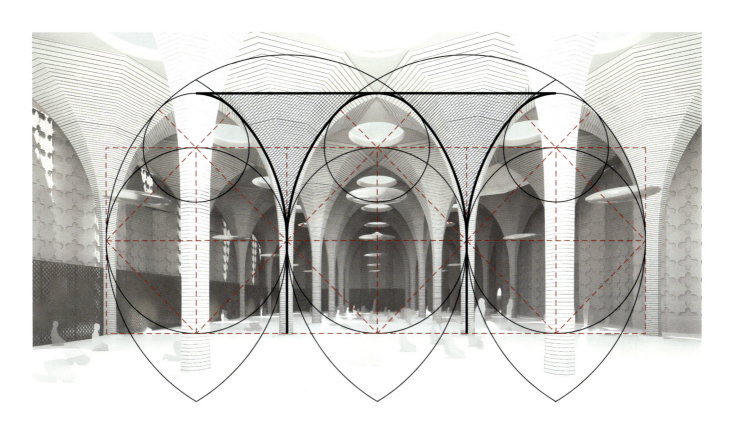

KEITH CRITCHLOW AND THE SACRED ART OF GEOMETRY

The marquetry patterns on the principal doors

(OVERLEAF) The marquetry patterns on the principal doors were based on the bespoke geometric design by Keith Critchlow.

KEITH CRITCHLOW AND THE SACRED ART OF GEOMETRY

In 2011, it was decided that the pattern should be diamond-shaped... Matters were made all the more challenging because there were pauses between one stage of the creation of the building and the next so that more funding could be found – in 2015, for example, there was a pause of two years. What the eye reads now as simplicity and clarity were arrived at with great difficulty, through the project's long evolution, with many stages of an immense complexity.

There is something marvellously wayward and maverick about Keith Critchlow's solutions to these abstruse sacred mysteries. Perhaps his own singular practice helps to explain and to illustrate why so few architectural production drawings of Islamic buildings have ever been discovered. Perhaps it has ever been so, this matter of trusting that the expert moving hand is in harmony with the archetypes controlling the rhythms of the heavens.

Cambridge Council required that 1 per cent of the building's budget be devoted to art, with a preference for it to be integrated into the building. In this case, Keith's contribution meant that the embellishment, by intricate marquetry, of doors and grilles, the tiling of the atrium floor and the pattern of the dome, could also, without a second's hesitation, qualify as works of art. The geometry of this building, and how it plays itself out, with such deftness, poise and rhythmical assurance, across its surfaces, gives Cambridge Central Mosque a beauty unlike that of most other mosques in the United Kingdom. It establishes a new architectural idiom for a sacred building, which feels both timely and timeless.

(ABOVE) Decorative screen in front portico, original pattern design by Keith Critchlow

(OPPOSITE) *Mashrabiya* screen designed by Marks Barfield Architects based on the geometric patterns by Keith Critchlow

(OPPOSITE) Stained glass designed by Keith Critchlow

(BELOW) Natural air vent in the prayer hall, pattern designed by Keith Critchlow

KEITH CRITCHLOW AND THE SACRED ART OF GEOMETRY   61

THE TREES! THE TREES!

(OVERLEAF) Cambridge
Central Mosque prayer hall

'What is it about this mosque which especially speaks to you?', I ask Shahida Rahman, a novelist and one of the trustees of Cambridge Central Mosque (there are four trustees in the United Kingdom, and a second female trustee in Turkey). She meets me in the late afternoon, fresh from her job at the Cambridge University Press. 'The mosque's most important feature? It is the trees, the trees', she tells me as we talk together in the cafe.[1] One of a family of five children, Shahida was born in 1961, the year that Bangladesh came into being as an independent nation, in the maternity hospital which once stood next to this building. The Bangladeshi Muslim community, which first began to establish itself here in the 1940s, is the largest in Cambridge. Her father arrived in 1957 and set to work as a cleaner while her mother remained in what was then East Pakistan. Later on, the family was reunited in Cambridge. It was responsible for opening two Asian restaurants in Regent Street, the first of their kind in the city.

Shahida's first experience of worship was during the middle years of the 1970s, in a house-mosque at 175 Chesterton Road. Friday prayers were celebrated in the living room with around 20 worshippers. She herself learnt Arabic from an Egyptian teacher. Now her local mosque is a place of pilgrimage for Muslims from all over the world. To Shahida, though, it remains thoroughly local, a place of homecoming.

The calming prayer hall is my favourite place after home. And the trees are its most special element. I also appreciate the fact that I have been involved with the project at every stage in its making, that my voice has been an important one to be listened to – you can see photographs of me wearing a yellow hard hat on-site when Cambridge Central Mosque was still nothing more than a building site!

Everything was open to discussion. Nothing was off bounds:

At first, there was talk of the garden being at the back of the mosque, and then the thinking evolved. All we locals felt involved in the decision-making process at all times. We helped to shape it, to make it what it is. It was to be our mosque . . . We always felt ourselves to be a part of it.

Shahida's industry within the local communities extends far beyond the boundaries of these four walls, I discover: her work with Macmillan Cancer Support, which includes regular coffee mornings at the mosque to raise awareness of cancer amongst the local community; volunteering at the local hospice; her charity work with Wintercomfort, which provides food and shelter to the needy; and her own charity, the Karim Foundation, which helps to relieve local poverty by distributing food, providing help with domestic costs and dealing with emergencies of various kinds. Her work caters for and reaches out to all, she is at pains to point out, regardless of background.

THE TREES! THE TREES!   63

(BELOW AND OVERLEAF)
Marks Barfield Architects,
axonometric concept layers

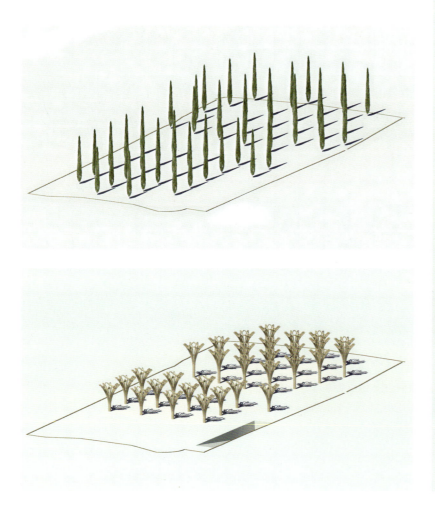
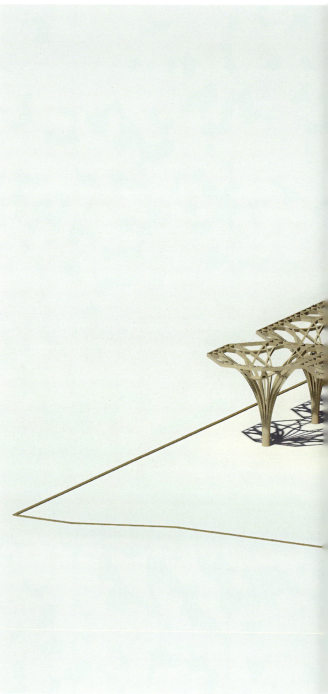

66 CAMBRIDGE CENTRAL MOSQUE

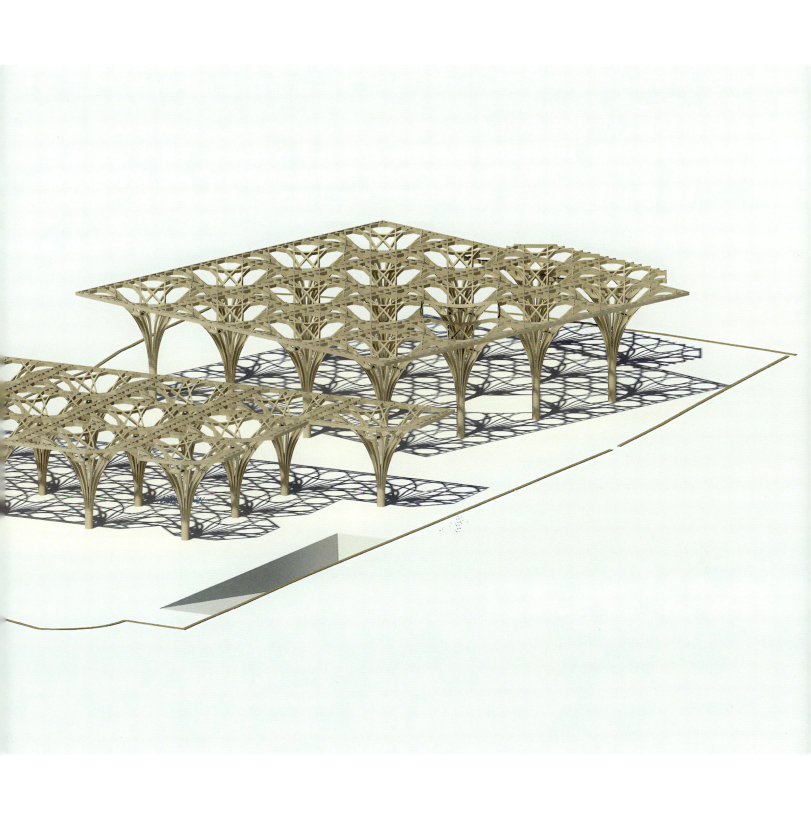

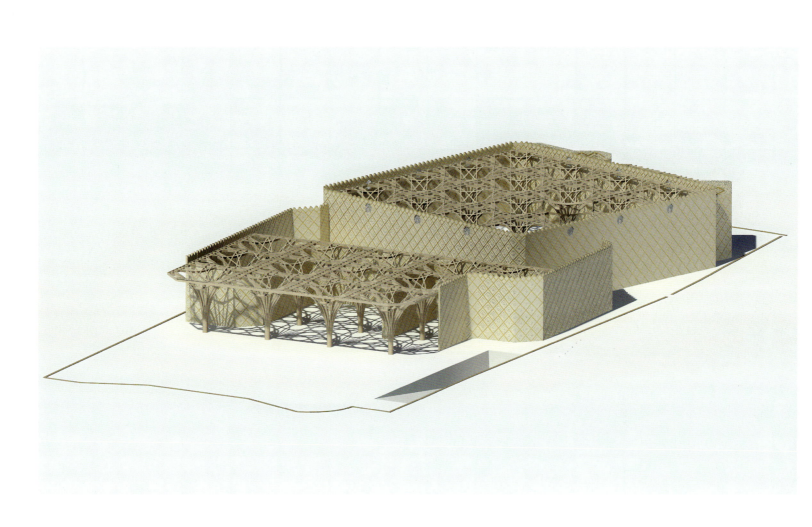

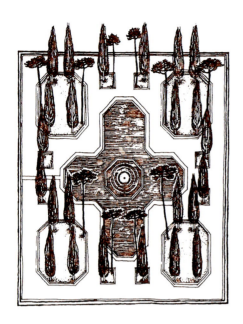

Inspirational image of an archetypical garden of paradise: courtyard plan of the Shrine of Sayyid Ni'matullah Wali, Mahan – 'here in the walled creation of man an order is traced in the garden floor by the structure waterways that flow from the highest to the lowest point, distributing the life-generating water to the various geometric compartments of the garden, the verdant, spontaneous growths contained within the garden compartments complement and balance the whole conception, which is viewed archetypically as the recapitulation of paradise'. Nader Ardalan and Laleh Bakhtiar, *The Sense of Unity: The Sufi Tradition in Persian Architecture* (University of Chicago Press: Chicago, IL, 1973)

'So much of what we do is about breaking down boundaries, of making all feel welcome and a part of something larger, which includes, of course, the fact that women and men pray together in the same prayer hall.'

It is the trees in the prayer hall to which she often returns as a subject of conversation. 'Yes, it is this calming prayer hall, I must emphasise, which is my most special place. And this is where I grew up. It is my local mosque . . .' And it is these fabricated trees which indeed most ravish the eye, from the moment you first see them in the overhanging portico, the covered space which overlooks the Islamic garden, to the prayer hall, by which time they have risen in height from 6 to 8 m, as if proximity to the holiest of Islamic places might have encouraged an extraordinary spurt of growth.

The idea of the symbolic tree has always been deep-rooted in the religion of Islam. According to *sura* 53:13–18, it was on the night of his ascension that the Prophet reached the enigmatic Tree of Heaven, when he received the instruction to inaugurate the five daily prayers of Islam. Elsewhere we are told that the trees and the stars prostrate to God. The Verse of Light (*sura* 24:35) mentions the olive tree; *sura* 14:24 recounts the parable of the goodly tree; Jonah, in *sura* 37:146, has his gourd tree. Trees are clearly heaven-sent, and have heavenly aspirations.

The trees at Cambridge Central Mosque were made on earth, and they are a triumph of traditional craftsmanship in combination with high technology. It was David Marks who first imagined the idea of a calm oasis of contemplation within a grove of trees. After much searching, he found Blumer Lehmann, a family-owned company (for five generations) in the town of Gossau, north-east Switzerland, whose factory is powered by wood offcuts and is completely self-sufficient. In his opinion, this was the best candidate to make the symbolic trees on which the success of the mosque's central idea – that all religious groupings, irrespective of caste or creed, could unite in homage to nature – so much depended. Blumer Lehmann were by no means the most competitive from a financial point of view, but they were undoubtedly the best for the job.

The example of the great mosque at Córdoba helped to inform their decision to use a grove of trees as the building's unifying element, Julia Barfield tells me.

In that building the forest of columns inside the mosque is continued into the outside, where you emerge into a forest of real trees, the symbolic linking hands with the natural world . . . Nature is universal. Everyone can revere nature, irrespective of creed or caste . . . Nature, not being a

70 CAMBRIDGE CENTRAL MOSQUE

Córdoba Mosque, Spain

doctrine open to varieties of interpretation, is not divisive. In fact, it is inclusive, universally so . . .[2]

Equally important as a point of departure was an image which she and David Marks discovered in a book called *A Sense of Unity: The Sufi Tradition in Persian Architecture* by Nader Ardalan and Laleh Bakhtiar. It showed a plan of a courtyard in Mahan of the shrine of Sayyid Ni'matullah Wali, a sacred space defined and enclosed and enveloped by a grove of trees.

But the trees of Cambridge Central Mosque posed huge challenges to their makers and designers. 'The fact that the structural elements were often required to curve in two directions was an issue with which we and Blumer Lehmann wrestled', Julia tells me as we stare together at a colourful digital working drawing of a tree.

They are almost equal in complexity to a spider's web . . . where each thread has a particular structural recipe related to its function in the web. As with the trees, each element is fabricated to respond to its specific structural role. We succeeded, finally, because of the strength of our teamwork. Architects are not artists. They are not loners. Architecture is collaborative, a team effort . . .

Blumer Lehmann will be celebrating the 150th anniversary of the establishment of the company in 2025. The project manager responsible for the Cambridge Central Mosque, Jephtha Schaffner, tells the story when we talk together in the Marks Barfield Architects offices in Clapham.[3] Blumer Lehmann's involvement with the project began in 2012, and continued for six years in all. The job was finished, the timber trees themselves installed on-site in Cambridge, at the end of January 2018, one month before the scheduled completion date. As with the architects, this was the first time that Blumer Lehmann had worked on a mosque. 'The difference, for us, was the strictness of the geometry, and how crucial it

THE TREES! THE TREES! 71

(BELOW AND OPPOSITE) Colour-coded three-dimensional digital model showing all the different structural elements and jointing details of the Cambridge Central Mosque tree structure.

72 CAMBRIDGE CENTRAL MOSQUE

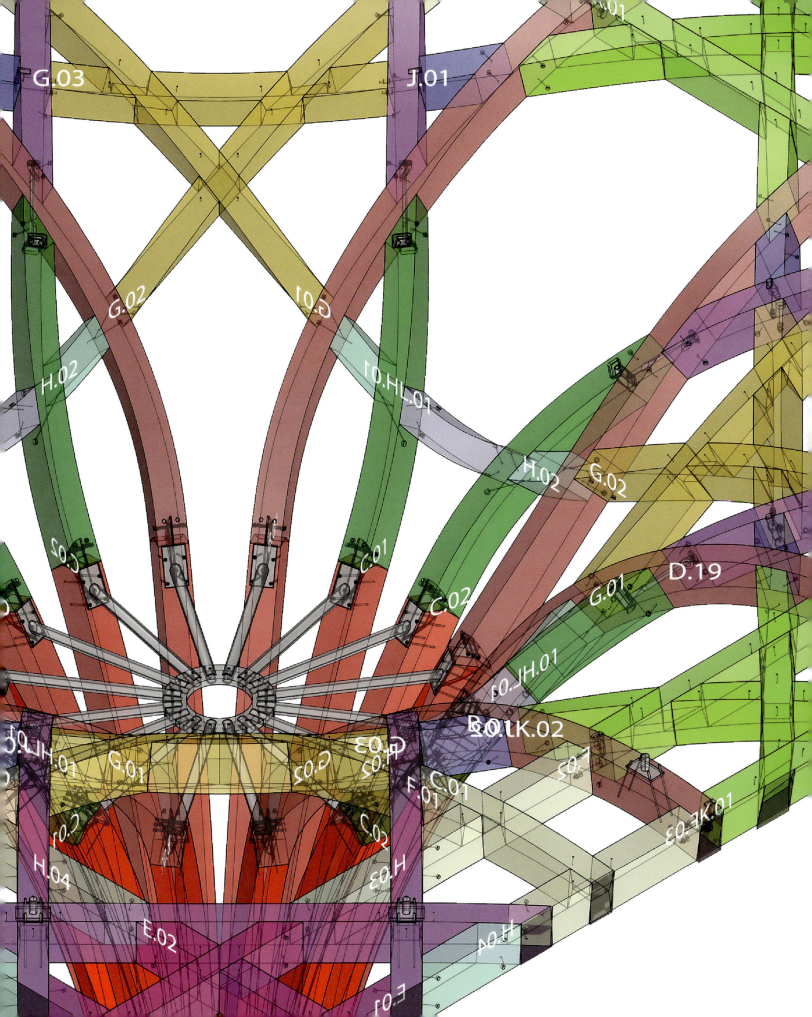

Blumer Lehmann staff dressed up for the topping out ceremony – when the preassembled dome, the highest feature, was lifted into place – on 30 November 2017

was for us to respect its rigours', explains Jephtha:

> this was what made the project very exciting for us. Otherwise, it did not deviate greatly from other projects. There was nervousness, of course, about whether or not it would be acceptable to the local community because what we were doing was so radical. Luckily, there was a great deal of ongoing consultation – Tim Winter saw to that. The project succeeded because there was such close cooperation at all times between all parties. There was a great deal of mutual respect.

The fabricated timber trees are all made from sustainably sourced spruce trees selected from forests within about 100 km of the Blumer Lehmann factory – though some came from as far north as the Frankfurt area. It required about 1600 trees to make the 30 that we see at the mosque. Generally speaking, a tree is felled when it has absorbed as much carbon as it is capable of absorbing.

The chosen trees were probably between 50 and 100 years old, and they would have been chosen from a forest containing a variety of species. There is not a lot of monoculture in Central Europe. At its best a sustainable forest contains trees of varying ages, older next to younger, so that when you fell an older tree, you clear space for the younger tree to mature by taking the taller old ones away.

Once back at the factory, they are dried – first outdoors, and then in a climate chamber – until they contain about 12 per cent moisture. At the point of felling, the moisture content could have been as high as 50 per cent. Then they are sliced into lamellas (thin slices or strips) of a thickness of 45 mm, planed, and glued together, one on top of another, to the requisite size. 'The timber is strong along the fibre, but not in the other direction' – Jephtha makes a gesture with his hands, crossing one of them over the other across the tabletop at which we are sitting in order to dramatise what would have happened in the factory – 'which is unlike, say,

74 CAMBRIDGE CENTRAL MOSQUE

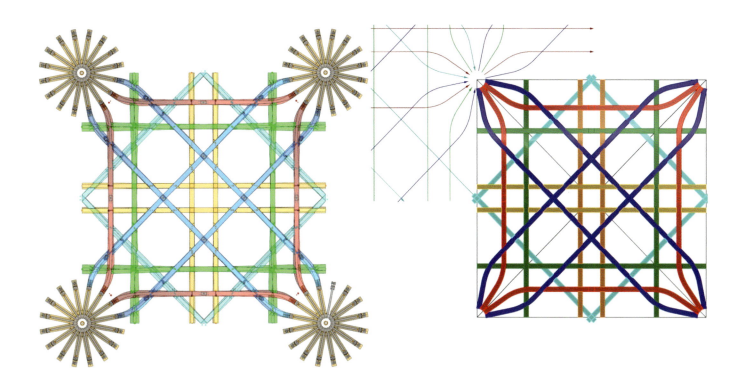

TYPE	TASK	LATEST VERSION	CONCEPT VERSION
Red:	Main Beam	4 piece	20 pieces
Dark Blue:	Main Beam	12 pieces	20 pieces
Light Blue:	Secondary Beam	20 pieces	8 pieces
Green:	Secondary Beam	28 pieces	20 pieces
Orange:	Secondary Beam	28 pieces	20 pieces
		92 pieces	**88 pieces**

(ABOVE) Blumer Lehmann, structure concept

(BELOW) Blumer Lehmann, structure concept

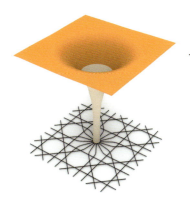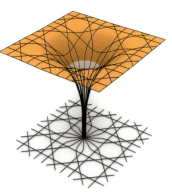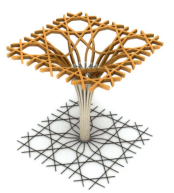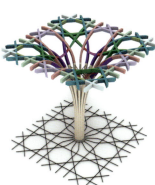

THE TREES! THE TREES!

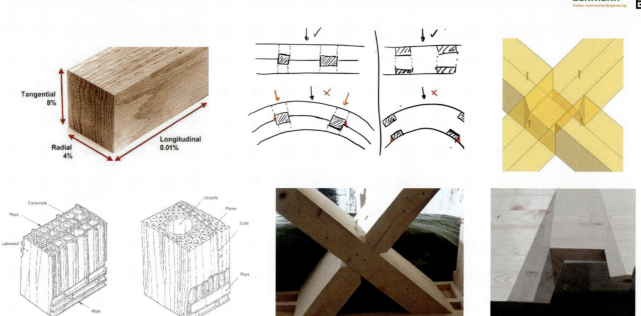

Blumer Lehmann, Junctions – halving joints

steel'. (The process will have reduced 50 per cent of the original tree to sawdust, but that sawdust will not go to waste and can be reconstituted as fibre, pallets, or used by the paper industry.)

Now you have a laminated timber blank. Some of these blanks are straight. Others will need to be single-curved, yet others double-curved. If the blank is to be curved, the lamellas will need to be thinner. The shapes and how they all interweave and interlock are determined by the rigour of the predetermined geometry, which the operator of the computer numerical control machine will need to follow as closely as is humanly possible. 'To accurately interpret this free-form geometry, it is necessary to be precise to within one half of a millimetre', Jephtha tells me. The entire project was an extraordinary exercise in close analytical work over a period of about eight months, a marrying of the talents of architects, structural engineers, designers and craftsmen. Around 20 people were involved in the design process in London, and there were 100 working in production in the factory in Switzerland to ensure that everything was coordinated in a timely fashion. 'It had to fit together like Lego', says Jephtha.

Once completed, the trees, in all their numbered constituent parts, were wrapped in plastic and shipped directly to their destination in Cambridge, 1500 km away to the west, in truck-load after truck-load – 80 in all, carrying approximately 3800 individual components. When the first truck arrived, the delivery site had not been concreted over, and it was finally

(BELOW) Blumer Lehmann, halving joints, 3 of 6000 connections

(BOTTOM) Blumer Lehmann, beam types. Straight and single curved beams were layered, whereas the double curved assembly beams were a checkerboard construction.

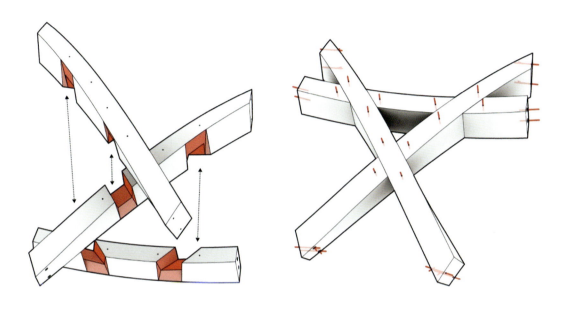

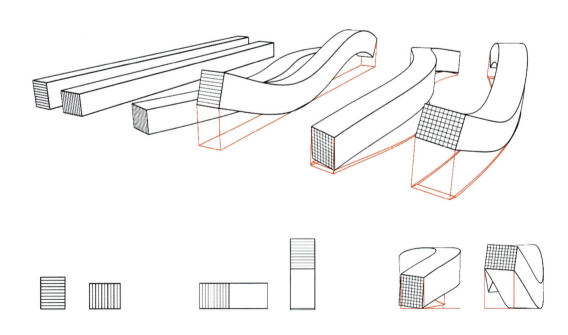

(BELOW) Timber blanks stacked ready for milling and assembly

(BOTTOM) Diagram showing the differing forms of beams after milling. Blanks shown in red

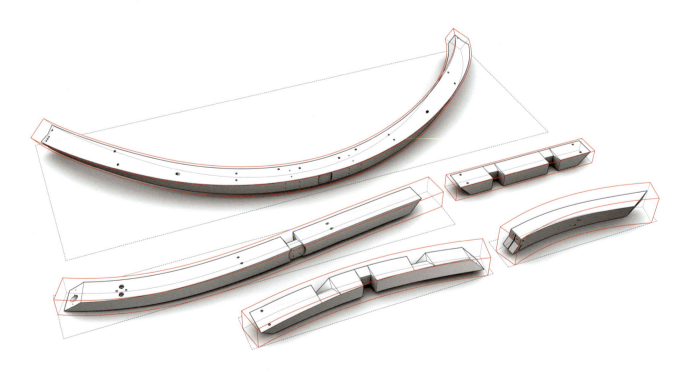

78   CAMBRIDGE CENTRAL MOSQUE

Beam and tree construction and milling process in the factory at different stages

THE TREES! THE TREES!

Stacks of milled beams

able to drive into position on the site after a week's delay. Six months were allocated to the job of assembling all the elements off-site, and then all these numbered components had to arrive in the correct order – adhering strictly to the correct sequencing was of crucial importance.

'It was the first time this kind of construction was created on quite this scale', Tim Winter comments.

> There was no company in the United Kingdom that could actually fabricate such cross-laminated, double curved trees. It was very unusual and very cutting-edge – in fact, you could call it off-the-wall if you like. Blumer Lehmann were undoubtedly more expensive, yes, but they proved that they could do it by, for example, making mock-ups of different sections so that we could appraise the trees in the making. Nothing was left to chance. And everything depended upon the success of these trees for the success of the project in its entirety because the spiritual solace of this grove of symbolic trees was the central idea of the Cambridge Mosque. And these trees were made by traditional craftsmanship working in combination with hi-tech skills and mathematical precision. Everything had to be slotted together without showing invisible cracks. And every component was transported, by lorry, to the site. Nothing happened on-site for six months. And then, after that time lag, walls and trees were all up within three weeks. It was almost a prefabricated building . . .[4]

(RIGHT) The beams packed and ready to go

(BELOW) A jig was made on-site to assemble the crowns that linked the trees.

THE TREES! THE TREES! 81

(LEFT) Crown and trunk junction

(BELOW) A crown with overlaid 'breath of the compassionate' pattern

(OPPOSITE) Naturally lit prayer hall in use during the COVID-19 pandemic with social distancing restrictions in place

82   CAMBRIDGE CENTRAL MOSQUE

SUSTAINABILITY

From the outset, the brief for the mosque called for a sustainable response in its widest sense, both social and environmental. As Tim Winter observed, 'A minimal carbon footprint is required to emphasise spiritual beliefs in humanity's role as a humble and responsible custodian of creation.'[1] We have already seen that Marks Barfield Architects has been committed to creating sustainable buildings from its inception. There was therefore a total alignment between client and design team.

Cambridge Central Mosque has been described as Europe's first eco-mosque, the first mosque to take the issue of climate change with the utmost seriousness, and endeavour to reduce its carbon footprint to as close to zero as possible. This ambition proved to be a challenge to some of the funders from the Middle East. How could a prayer hall packed with worshippers possibly function without air conditioning? The goal was both practical and theological. The building had to set itself the task of being an exemplar of environmentally friendly practice – and making the point that Islam abhors waste, and believes human beings to be set on the earth to be its environmentally responsible custodians.

Sustainability is at the heart of a conversation with Matthew Wingrove,[2] the project architect from the Marks Barfield team who had day-to-day responsibility for the mosque as it was under construction. Much of the mosque is timber, which 'is the ideal construction material, workable, manageable, versatile, lighter than steel or concrete', Matthew points out. Ideal from the point of view of sustainability, too

– wood is embodied carbon. In sustainably managed forests of Central Europe of the kind from which the spruce trees used in the fabricated trees of this building came, the goal is to take down the living tree once it has absorbed as much carbon as possible, and then to put a new young tree in its place so that the cycle can begin again.

Timber has so many advantages from the human point of view too. It feels close to us in a way that metal and concrete do not. It is soft acoustically, and warm to the touch. Who does not take pleasure in sitting on a wooden bench? It does not become waste. It is reparable: a wooden structure, if well looked after, will last for hundreds of years. So unlike concrete, that man-made material, which cracks and turns ugly so soon. But wood is the principal building material for another reason too. The words of David Marks, written some years before, were cited when it won the Wood Awards in 2019: 'This building is an exemplar of how wood can enable a structure to become the primary representational element of a building . . . Wood does not simply represent sustainability and warmth: it also reflects the thinking that underpins the structure.'[3]

Yes, timber embodies the guiding idea of the mosque as a natural habitat insofar as it consists of a grove of trees. You recognise the preponderance of wood immediately from the interior, but a little less so when you walk around its exterior walls, which appear to be made from brick, patterned and highlighted by quotations from the Qur'an. All is not quite as it seems

SUSTAINABILITY   85

(LEFT) Blumer Lehmann, cross-laminated timber wall panels

(OPPOSITE TOP) Marks Barfield Architects, Sustainability principles

(OPPOSITE BELOW) Marks Barfield Architects, Long section of Cambridge Central Mosque

though. There are older traditions of local fabrication at work here too. In the 18th and 19th centuries, many East Anglian buildings were constructed from a timber frame with brick tiles clipped deftly on top. That local tradition has been followed here. The brick is of the surface only. All these brick tiles are held in place by a timber framework.

The challenges of making this building sustainable were huge. How to keep it warm enough in the winter and cool enough in the summer without generating energy by traditional means? It is a sacred space with a capacity for 1000 worshippers in the prayer hall. 'In practice, that means, given the patterns of public worship, that we have a building that is used at only 5 per cent of its capacity much of the time', explains Mark Maidment, from Skelly & Couch, who joined the team as a design consultant in

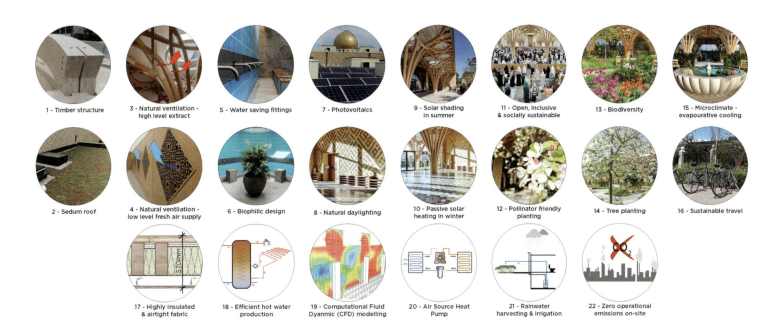

1 - Timber structure
2 - Sedum roof
3 - Natural ventilation - high level extract
4 - Natural ventilation - low level fresh air supply
5 - Water saving fittings
6 - Biophilic design
7 - Photovoltaics
8 - Natural daylighting
9 - Solar shading in summer
10 - Passive solar heating in winter
11 - Open, inclusive & socially sustainable
12 - Pollinator friendly planting
13 - Biodiversity
14 - Tree planting
15 - Microclimate - evapourative cooling
16 - Sustainable travel
17 - Highly insulated & airtight fabric
18 - Efficient hot water production
19 - Computational Fluid Dyanmic (CFD) modelling
20 - Air Source Heat Pump
21 - Rainwater harvesting & irrigation
22 - Zero operational emissions on-site

SUSTAINABILITY 87

sustainability and mechanical engineer in 2011, eight years before the building opened to the public.[4] The team also benefited from the advice of the highly experienced engineer Loren Butt, a long-term Marks Barfield Architects advisor who suggested from the outset that the site should be fossil-fuel free. How to make it both comfortable to use and environmentally friendly? How to create a building that would use as little energy as possible and take maximum advantage of passive heating? How to create a sustainably managed environment that would rise to the challenge of the level of occupancy required of it during the month of Ramadan?

The solutions were radical. 'The building has almost nothing in the way of thermal mass, which means that its capacity to release or store heat energy is almost self-regulating', explains Mark. 'The building took very seriously indeed the year-on-year decarbonisation of the grid.' There is no gas or oil on site, and no air conditioning. Good insulation and air-tight construction mean that no heating is wasted, and there is no loss or gain of heat from ill-fitting doors. Air source heat pumps extract heat from the air. Sensors attached to the energy-efficient light fittings monitor intensity of light inside the building, activating dimmers when necessary. An array of photovoltaic screens on the roof (donated by a local Cambridge Muslim business which supplies green technologies to Morocco and Saudi Arabia) offsets up to 30 per cent of the building's electricity use. 'We would have liked to install

even more of them, but the timber roof structure would not sustain the weight. We had to move them around several times', Mark comments. Rainwater is harvested from the roof, collected in the basement, and reused to flush the toilets and irrigate the garden.

'All the main public spaces are naturally lit and naturally ventilated', Julia Barfield tells me as we walk around the mosque together. 'The building is designed with enough natural light to make it possible to do without the need to put on any electric lights during the day. CO_2 monitors regulate air quality. It is all about minimising the amount of energy needed, and keeping the running costs down.'[5] All this natural light floods in through the circular oculi or skylights, which are positioned above every one of the trees inside the building – 44 of them in all. Even the ablution areas have them.

An enormous amount of work went into calculating the height and the diameter of those roof lights – we needed to let in as much light as possible, but avoid admitting heat. Air comes in at a low level, and leaves at a much higher level through the vents surrounding the skylights. There is a great deal of natural daylight, but no direct sunlight.

There are vents that suck out air at a much lower level too – concealed behind the decorative grilles in the prayer hall and elsewhere. Hot air generated at this level rises and is then sucked out through air ducts. Fans can be activated at a higher level to pull hot air out, should that be

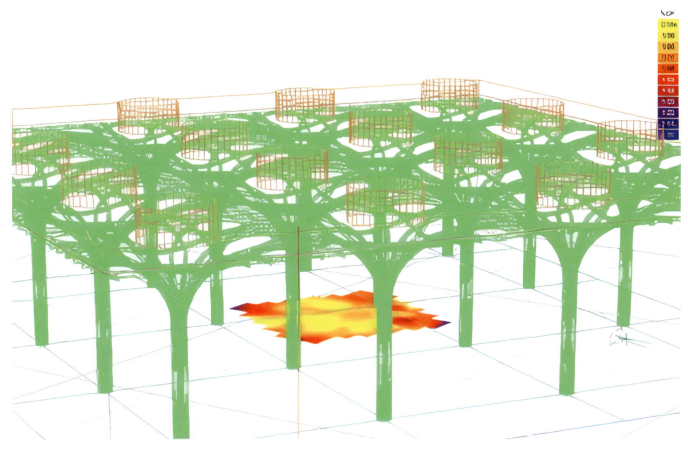

(ABOVE) Skelly & Couch,
Natural light analysis mode

(RIGHT) Skelly & Couch,
Natural light analysis grid

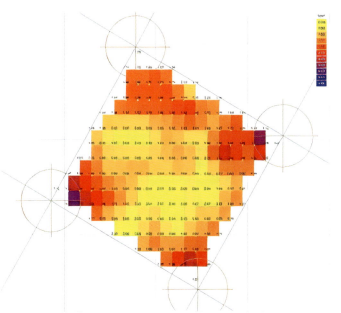

Skelly & Couch,
Natural ventilation heatmap

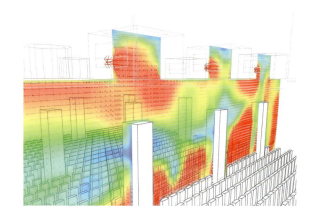

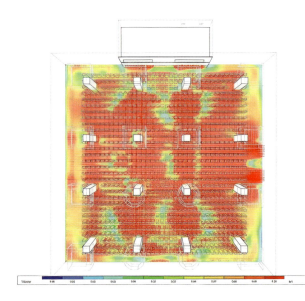

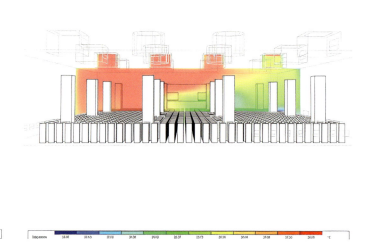

needed at moments of maximum occupancy. One of the best ways of recognising how the natural light works hand in hand with the means of ventilation is to shin up a ladder on to the roof above the prayer hall, and see the unexpected presence of the giant white boxes that enclose the skylights and contain these fans. All this extraction of air does not come without a degree of noise pollution, of course, and so in order to prevent the roar of heat extraction blighting the neighbourhood, an acoustic wall has been built on the lower roof between the atrium and the prayer hall, well out of human sight.

As I walk into the portico, I notice that a young man has been careful to ensure that the great glazed door through which I have just passed has closed properly behind me. Discussion of the importance of doors and how they fit are particularly pressing matters as any project inches towards its conclusion. Are the angles correct? Do the doors hang as they should? Does a pair of doors meet in the middle, and if the marquetry is divided between one door and its partner, does the eye jump across the void satisfactorily to complete the visual pattern? Doors are such a key element in a sacred space such as this one, Matthew Wingrove explains to me; they 'need to be robust, strong, un-flimsy because they are in continuous use'.[6] The doors of a mosque are of great symbolic importance too. 'If they are doing their job, they will provide a sense of entry that is almost ritualistic.' You will feel their weight as you gently push against them. Weight carries with it a measure of authority. 'They will be perceived as a significant threshold, and especially if they are decorated with meaningful marquetry, as these doors are.' The patterning and the veneer are designed to be objects of solemn contemplation in their own right. The doors must have a certain grandeur about them, grandeur in tandem with strength and durability. The hinges and handles matter greatly too. Are they strong enough?

Door handles have to prove their value too – they cannot be flimsy, which is tantamount to un-serious. One early prototype snapped off. The ones chosen for the mosque have a brass-coated finish so that they will be seen to be in harmony with other features of the building. All must work together as a whole . . . A sense of unity and uniformity is so important.

The fit and the patterning of the carpet were also matters of crucial importance. Does the foot of each tree meet the edge of the carpet in the prayer hall exactly as it needs to? The pattern gives out a message about the use of personal space, how worshippers are being encouraged to organise themselves in relation to each other – this was especially important during the COVID-19 years. The patterning of the carpet is repeatedly interrupted by the procession of trees – it is almost as if they erupt out of the carpet, by some miracle. How to deal with this stop-and-start patterning so that harmony and a continuing sense of visual flow are maintained?

All these elements have to work together, and be seen to be harmoniously combined,

within an environment which is almost self-regulating. There are no windows at ground level at all in the prayer hall. The dappled sunlight admitted through the roof lights is experienced through the secondary reflections that play on the white walls. A sustainable environment such as this one, you appreciate as you stand and contemplate everything that surrounds you, induces calmness and a certain centring of the self.

WELCOME TO THE MOSQUE: A TOUR INTO THE HEART OF THE SACRED

It's a cheerful, early May day, and the train has arrived on time. Sayedur Rahman, my affable taxi driver, seems to know the route from Cambridge station to the mosque very well, and the journey takes a matter of minutes. 'I live nearby', he tells me. 'Many years I have lived here.' And this mosque? How did he find it? 'I often come here to pray', he says, 'it's very convenient. It is very open, very welcoming. I come here all the time.'[1]

'How a building roots itself in a place is always so important', Gemma Collins, the former director of Marks Barfield Architects who oversaw the mosque during the technical and construction phases of the project, and is currently the custodian of all 17 buildings which comprise the parliamentary estate, explains to me. 'The mosque sits so well within Romsey Town, that residential area of south-east Cambridge – the way that it meets the street; how the materials from which it is fabricated seem to blend with the local; its scale inside and out; the walk through . . .'[2] We are meeting for a coffee in the atrium of Portcullis House, directly across the road from Big Ben. She looks admiringly up at the twist of the glulam beams just above our heads and the glazed ceiling, linking in her mind an important feature of Michael Hopkins's building at the heart of historic London, and the glulam beams that twist across the roof of the prayer hall, in a display of interlacing octagonal latticework, at the Cambridge Central Mosque.

In 2009 David Marks summarised in a note how important it was, when considering the impact of the new mosque, for it to be at one with its physical environment, both to respect it and to respond to it sympathetically:

> The mosque is set within a wider context, an urban landscape that has its own patterns, cultural traditions and character so that what we are seeking is a design that is true to itself, but also reflects or distils that character in which it will embed itself. The design becomes a receptacle of influence and condenses this culture so that hopefully what emerges is an English mosque true to British Muslim culture and recognisable British tradition.[3]

Cambridge Central Mosque, which is roughly on a north–south axis, is about twice as long as it is wide, and if you (as the hand of God) were to lift and place King's College Chapel directly on top of the site, it would make for a near-perfect fit. Those proportions are put to good use. The slow walk through the building feels like a journey (or even a grave processional) in several quite distinct stages, away from the frenetic secular busyness of the road, in the direction of the prayer hall, which marks a point of final homecoming, a space dedicated to inwardness and contemplation of the Divine.

King's College Chapel on the other side of town is an important point of reference for the mosque because of the way in which the chapel's 16th-century English fan-vaulting seems to be echoed in the trees of the mosque's prayer hall, in the way that they rise, both in

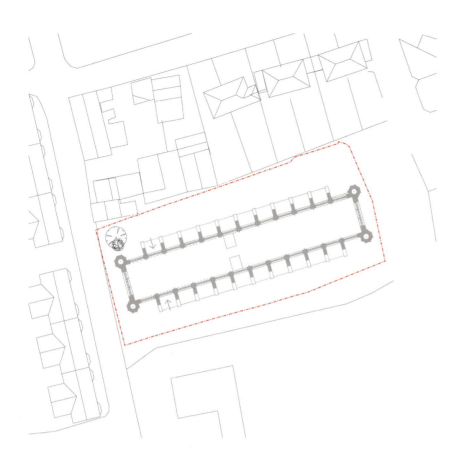

(LEFT) Marks Barfield Architects, Site plan showing King's College Chapel superimposed

(BELOW) Marks Barfield Architects, Cambridge Central Mosque model fitting in with the context

94　CAMBRIDGE CENTRAL MOSQUE

Marks Barfield Architects,
Cambridge Central Mosque plan

Ground Floor Plan

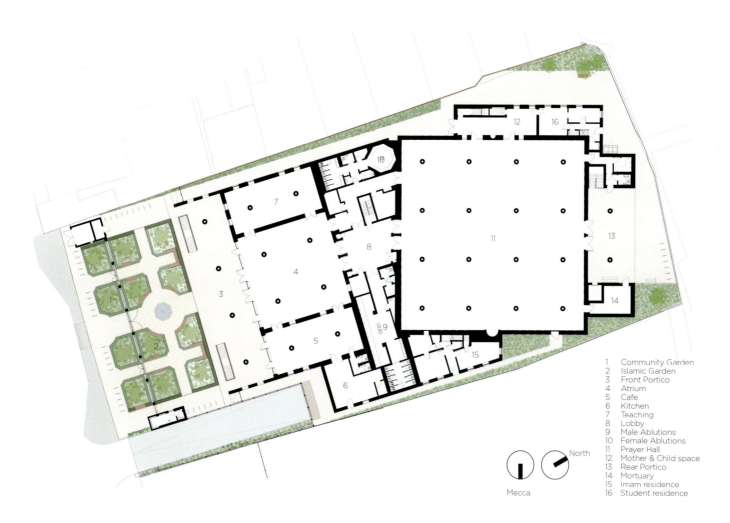

1 Community Garden
2 Islamic Garden
3 Front Portico
4 Atrium
5 Cafe
6 Kitchen
7 Teaching
8 Lobby
9 Male Ablutions
10 Female Ablutions
11 Prayer Hall
12 Mother & Child space
13 Rear Portico
14 Mortuary
15 Imam residence
16 Student residence

WELCOME TO THE MOSQUE: A TOUR INTO THE HEART OF THE SACRED   95

Fan vaulting in the Chapter House,
Westminster Abbey, London

support of the roof and seemingly in supplication too, the practical blending neatly with the metaphorical – their shape, their symmetry, their positioning, the way they fan out into the air, as if uplifted in prayer and yearning. It is good to have this reference point to historic University of Cambridge, *alma mater* of Isaac Newton, John Milton and Stephen Hawking, in this part of the city. It helps to knit it all together in a great synthesis. There are other reference points in this building to historic Cambridge, which we will notice later on. It is also worth recalling that Gothic fan vaulting originates in Islamic architecture – as Diana Darke points out in *Stealing from the Saracens*.[4]

The prayer hall is the end-point of our journey through the mosque, which starts out on Mill Road itself, beside the relentlessly secular and workaday presence of the no.2 bus stop directly outside its entrance. The overhanging portico of the mosque is your first sight of the building from the street, as you peer through the double gates, and across the Islamic garden which precedes it. The building is set far back from the road, quite unobtrusively so, as if reluctant to declare itself too soon. The roofline of the mosque is crenulated, a small architectural indication of heavenward journeying – symbolising earth and heaven; solid and void. An inscription in Kufic script by Hüseyin Kutlu, a contemporary Turkish master calligrapher, is emblazoned across the front of the portico, and it reads, from right to left (these are Allah's words, from the Qur'an,

speaking to Moses from the Burning Bush): 'I am God, there is no God but me, so establish worship for my remembrance' (*sura* 20:14).

There is a little community garden outside the boundary wall, almost touching the bus stop. The mosque recedes back into itself, step by step, zone by zone. It is low-lying, hunkered down. What you do not fully appreciate on that first look is that it rises as it withdraws from us, and that it will have grown by a full 20 m by the time you have completed your journey by walking into the prayer hall. That discovery adds such drama to the encounter.

Its form out here in the urban landscape does not seek to dominate or to domineer. It does not so much rise and rear up as skim across from west to east. It is not stridently a mosque. There is no minaret to be seen, and no call to prayer to be heard out in the streets of Romsey Town. When the call to prayer happens, it does so discreetly, in front of the *mihrab* within the prayer hall itself, that sacred space which is furthest from the street. The small golden dome, set at the back of the building, is barely visible. The consequence is that the building does not look rebarbative or out of place. It is not a 'carbuncle' – to repeat the word that King Charles III once used of an architectural scheme for the proposed Sainsbury Wing of London's National Gallery which was later withdrawn.[5] It does not look threatening – or under threat by those who might be hostile to its presence here. It does not feel alien at all; in fact, it feels at home, well bedded down in Romsey Town. In the words of

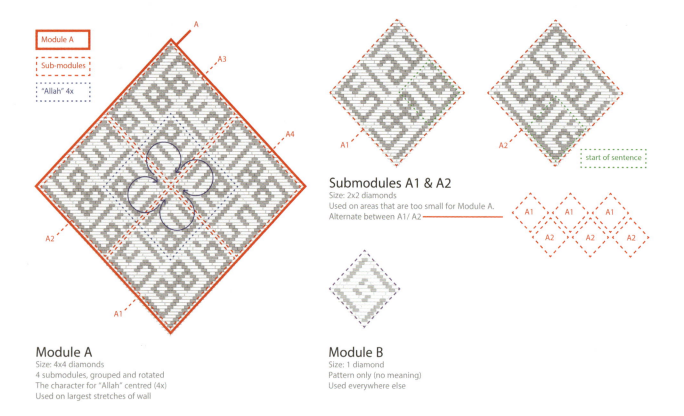

Module A
Size: 4x4 diamonds
4 submodules, grouped and rotated
The character for "Allah" centred (4x)
Used on largest stretches of wall

Submodules A1 & A2
Size: 2x2 diamonds
Used on areas that are too small for Module A.
Alternate between A1/ A2

Module B
Size: 1 diamond
Pattern only (no meaning)
Used everywhere else

David Marks: 'The aim was that the mosque should fit in and stand out at the same time.'[6]

The fact that what we see in front of our eyes is fabricated from brick and timber helps us to enjoy its presence. Timber always pleases. It has a warmth to it that even the eye recognises. What is more, the brick tiles clipped to the building's timber-framed boundary walls, a light buff in colour, remind us of the bricks of the 19th-century terraced housing that we passed in the taxi. They even have coloured highlights, as do some of the Victorian buildings just across the road. Seeing these bricks also reminds us of the fact that the making of this building has been an international endeavour. Although in colour, size and shape entirely characteristic of the look of 19th-century Cambridge, the bricks themselves were sourced from Germany because there was a shortage in the United Kingdom when they were needed. Some of the bricklayers who did the work of hanging them on-site were Montenegrin, others from the Baltic States.

The experience of the mosque itself, when we enter it, is a studiedly slow revelation. This is all to the good. Hurrying would diminish its impact. The journey is both physical and spiritual, into the heart of a building, and into the heart of ourselves. We do not fully understand its shape, its progress, or the possibility of its full impact, until we have walked right through it. Even though the building itself is set back from the road, it is perfectly aligned with the street's building line. This alignment helps it to blend, to look and to feel at one with that which surrounds it and that which it surrounds, the old and the not so old. This was not always the case. As with so much else, the idea of how the building should embed itself into its location changed over the years of its making.

Marks Barfield Architects, 'Kufic Calligraphy in Brickwork', brick cladding concept module A, used on the largest stretches of wall

(RIGHT) Soraya Syed, square Kufic calligraphy with central modules reading 'Say he is God, the One' as they rotate

(BELOW) Square Kufic calligraphy on exterior façade of the Ulugh Beg Madrasa, Samarkand, Uzbekistan

WELCOME TO THE MOSQUE: A TOUR INTO THE HEART OF THE SACRED

Cambridge University Real Tennis Club decorative brickwork wall.

In David Marks's very first rough drawing of 2008, in which he divides the space to be occupied into modules, it is not quite what it would become in the end. One of the few requirements is that the prayer hall's *qibla* wall should face Mecca. In that first drawing, the entire building is turned so that its long, right-hand wall is facing in that direction. This means that the mosque as then conceived would not have been aligned with the buildings of the street. Later, that plan would be modified in order to respect the earlier building line. The prayer hall alone now cants to the right, but nothing else does so before it – the modest change in direction is not visible until you encounter it at that point in your journey through the building.

But first it is the garden that we see – or I should say gardens because a double-gated boundary wall comes between the two gardens. It is at this boundary wall that we first appreciate that geometry will play a key role in the building. The capstones which crown the brick posts on either side of the double gates are polygonal, not the more familiar cannonball circular. There was no space for a larger garden, its co-designer, Emma Clark, tells me some days later when we talk together on a rainy afternoon at the British Library.[7] Emma, who teaches at the Prince's Foundation School of Traditional Arts, has designed Islamic gardens throughout the world, and she is the author of the standard book on the art of the Islamic garden. But despite the garden's small size, it feels like a gesture of beckoning and welcome, a way of inviting every member of the community into the mosque. It is also a respite. The first part of it, on the street side of the wall, is a community garden, and it is dominated by four birch trees. This May morning it is spilling out towards the road, quite riotously so in places, as if it is trying to claim new ground or catch a bus. There had been a birch tree on this spot in the past, and local residents didn't want to lose a species of tree of which they had grown so fond. They wanted that sense of connectedness with the past.

(BELOW) David Marks, early site sketch, 23 July 2009

(OVERLEAF) Marks Barfield Architects' design development plans (2009–2011) showing the key moves made to position the atrium and garden looking towards Mill Road while the prayer hall respects a focus towards Mecca

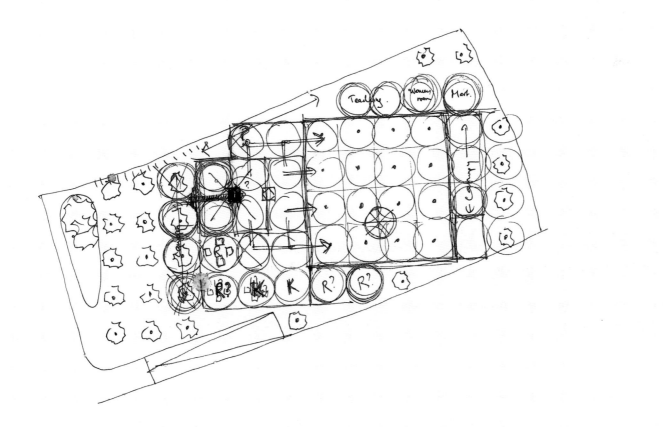

WELCOME TO THE MOSQUE: A TOUR INTO THE HEART OF THE SACRED 101

APRIL 2009 COMPETITION ENTRY

NOVEMBER 2010

102 CAMBRIDGE CENTRAL MOSQUE

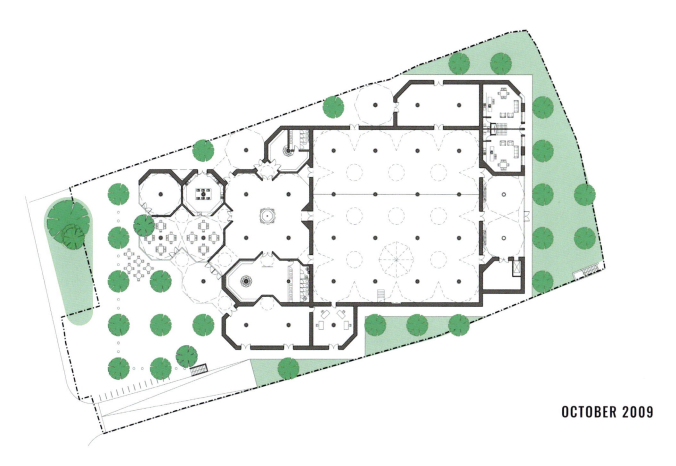

OCTOBER 2009

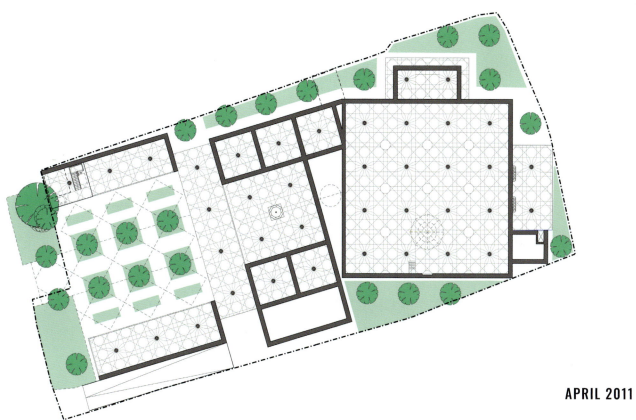

APRIL 2011

WELCOME TO THE MOSQUE: A TOUR INTO THE HEART OF THE SACRED   103

(BELOW) Marks Barfield Architects, site plan

Who tends this garden? Helen Seal, a professional gardener who once worked for Cambridge University Botanic Gardens, guides me through all the minutiae of garden-making and loving garden-tending that happens during the day that she works at the mosque. In fact, not quite a day, she tells me, with, I feel, a touch of regret.[8] Helen is here half a day every week, aided by a handful of enthusiastic volunteers, many of them from the Bangladeshi community. The community garden, she tells me, is planted with many herbaceous shrubs. Today it is a sight of teeming, close-packed, unpruned abundance. We look down at it, and, leaning forward, smell the commingled scents of rosemary and sage. As I take in the aromas, she is naming other favourites which are present here: Russian sage, Mexican fleabane, geraniums. Each of the 13 beds has been planted with bulbs – 750 in all. The railings that divide the community garden from the Islamic garden will eventually be covered in summer jasmine, which will give a degree of enclosure and set-apartness to the interior garden, and perhaps partially replicate the effect of an orange grove too, she tells me. The colour palette is blue, pink, purple and white, all colours which complement each other. She is very fond of tulip seed heads, she tells me, because they are redolent of Islamic design. You often see tulip shapes in 16th-century tiles native to Turkey and the Middle East. Her knowledge of garden lore needs no watering.

104 CAMBRIDGE CENTRAL MOSQUE

(BELOW) View of the mosque from Mill Road

(BOTTOM) Main entrance gates to the mosque with the public garden on the outside and the fountain and mosque garden on the inside

WELCOME TO THE MOSQUE: A TOUR INTO THE HEART OF THE SACRED

The community garden

We pass through the gates – they open to everyone at 10 o'clock in the morning – and into the Islamic garden proper, which looks and feels calmer and more strictly regulated than its town cousin beside the bus stop. This small garden does not attempt to replicate other Islamic gardens (and certainly not in its planting), but rather to offer certain features that such gardens might – and often do – contain. It is, in short, a garden respectful of Islamic tradition. The garden is divided into four segments, with paths between, which brings to mind the four rivers of heaven in the Paradise Gardens referred to in the Qur'an. Facing us as we enter is an octagonal stone fountain made from Portuguese limestone.

It is surrounded by four curved, handmade oak benches. The fountain, a perfect object of contemplation, brims with water continuously. The sound of water calms, soothes and delights. To a Muslim, flowing water is also a symbol of the soul. It spills over. It is eternally in motion.

The garden has a yew hedge at its back, which adds both a touch of geometric rigour and a sense of boundedness. It also reminds us of the yews to be found in so many English churchyards, which gives a reassuring sense of connectedness with the familiar. Crab apple trees have been planted, which means blossom in the spring, and fruit in late autumn. Tulips are here too, long, thin and elegant, and a lot of marjoram, a Mediterranean herb. 'The idea',

The central fountain

Helen explains, 'is that there will be a succession of flowers as we move through the seasons, sure proof that this is a dynamic garden of ever-changing display . . .' The ideal would be to have the whole ground covered with blooms . . .' Variety is important. 'All eight beds have the same plants, but we put them in different places. It is not a symmetrical planting.' The roses will be full of colour, deep pink to cerise, by and by. Then she frowns, momentarily. 'Soon the ladybirds will arrive to eat the aphids which are attacking the roses – look out for the orange eggs on the undersides of leaves – and stay calm!' She points out a mahaleb cherry tree from Iran, the giant oat grass (corn-white in colour) and the giant clover, which she describes as a 'good performer', more than capable of withstanding the British weather. 'We use seaweed as a plant invigorator or tonic – no chemicals!' She tells me about the plant nursery that she is developing, and how she is teaching her team of volunteers the art of taking cuttings. They are eager to grow vegetables too, and that may come in time, space permitting.

The grid of crab apple trees towards the back of the garden also prepares us for the symbolic grove of trees within the mosque itself, which is already spilling out into the shady, covered portico just beyond the garden's outermost edge. But before we approach the atrium, there is the rest of the garden to be considered.

THE GARDENS

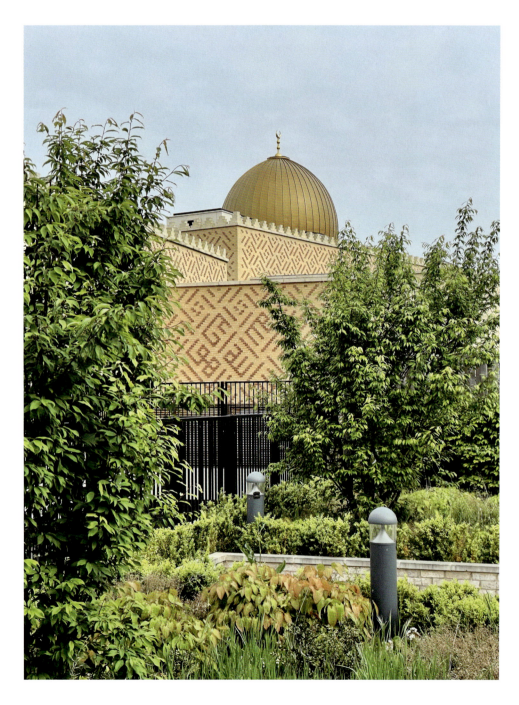

(LEFT) View of the dome from Mill Road

(OPPOSITE AND OVERLEAF) The mosque garden in the springtime

WELCOME TO THE MOSQUE: A TOUR INTO THE HEART OF THE SACRED 111

THE PORTICO

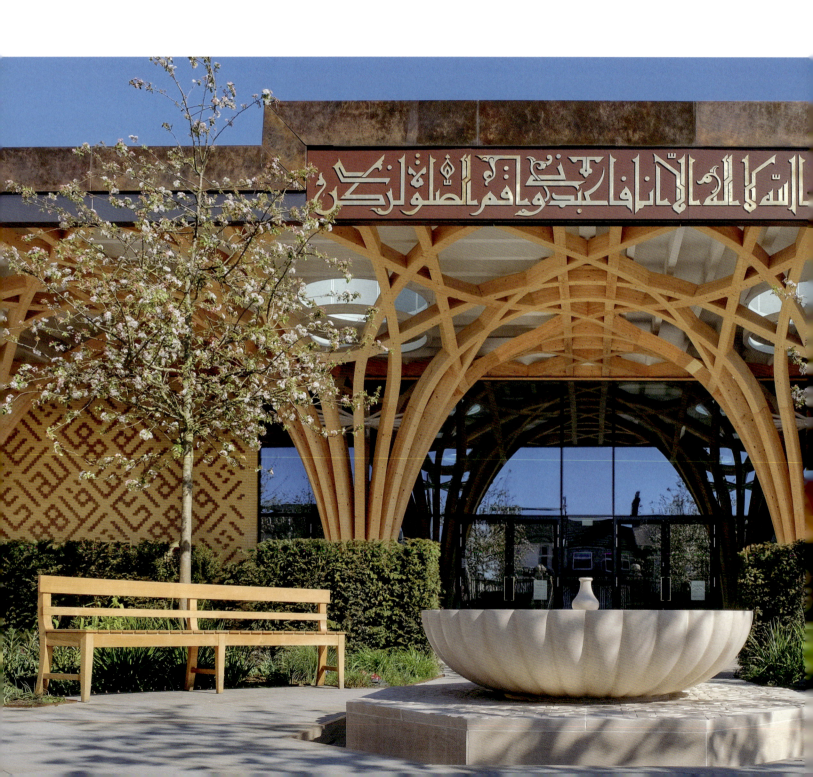

The Islamic garden fountain and front portico and mosque entrance

WELCOME TO THE MOSQUE: A TOUR INTO THE HEART OF THE SACRED

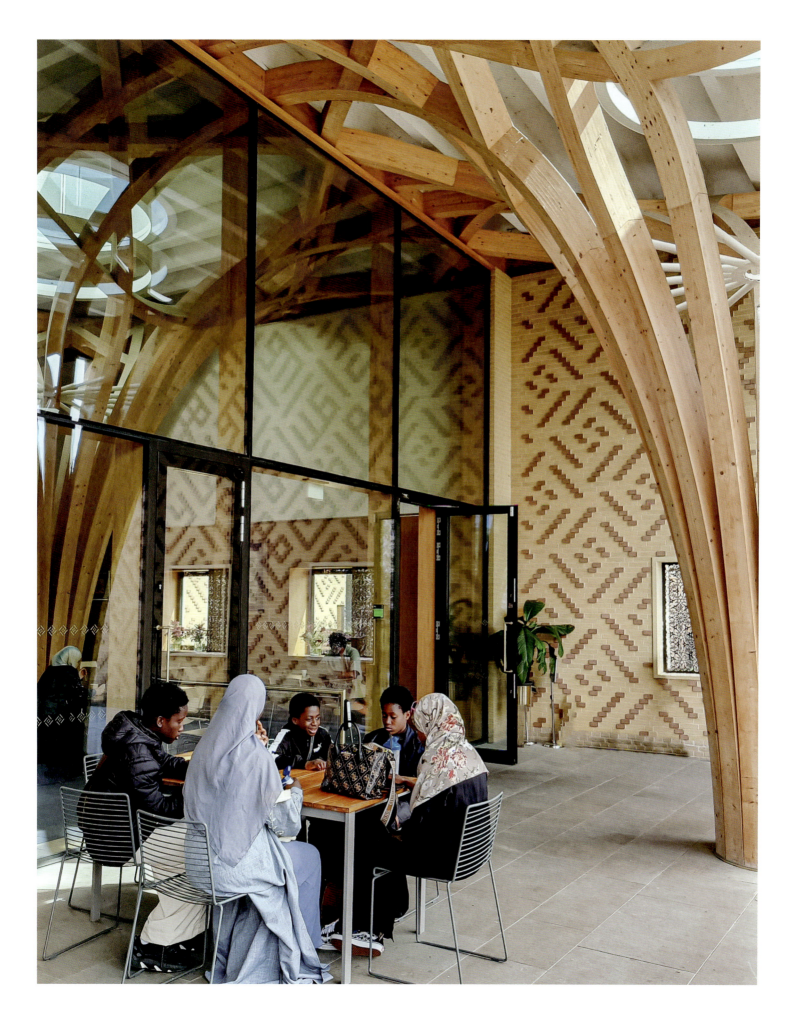

It continues around the sides and back of the building, a much narrower planting space, with a depth of soil of no more than 15 cm, but still of interest and importance. This is where a garden for children may take shape in the fullness of time.

'The idea of the Islamic garden includes the idea of enclosure', Emma Clark explains.[9]

The garden, which you enter straight from a very horrible and busy road, offers a respite, creates a sense of privacy, the calming effect of a going within. It marks a point of transition. Before you walk through the gates, you will see jasmine flowering. We wanted colours that would look beautiful together. The yew hedge at the back, an evergreen, gives a shape to the whole. In time the crab apples will rise to a good height so that they will line up with the columns. We wanted to avoid a Japanese look. It was important to keep the planting as native as possible, with sustainability in mind at all times. There is to be no use of pesticides, it all has to be looked after organically . . .

The planting had to be loose, not too formal. 'You hear the sound of water, flowing and spilling over, eternally, from the fountain – which was a very expensive feature.' The money was found, thanks to Tim Winter's fundraising efforts. 'The garden's four-fold form, with paths between the beds, echoes descriptions of the gardens of paradise that you can read in *sura* 55 of the Qur'an.' The idea was to give a taste of the Islamic world, but not to seek to replicate it in any way. 'In my view, this is the most beautiful mosque in the British Isles, and I feel honoured to be a part of it. So many mosques are so ugly. They have no conception of the beautiful. This one does. It is not a question of money. It is a question of aesthetics.'

The portico is where the outside moves towards the inside, where the civic continues its journey towards the innermost sanctum of the sacred. This is a meeting place for all, where people mill and gather. I have been walking and chatting with Ihsan, one of a number of volunteer tour guides – more and more of them are needed as the months go by – and the story of the mosque, its making and its presence here in east Cambridge, is told and retold. Ihsan is of Punjabi descent, and he grew up in Huddersfield. In 1981 he came south to Cambridge to study earth sciences at Darwin College, and here he has remained. 'In the year that I arrived in Cambridge, we prayed in the sitting room of a house at Mitcham's Corner, 20 or 30 of us. Now see what we have here today. There were 10,000 donors to this building, and visitors come from as far afield as Paris, Hyderabad and Bosnia. See how far we have come!'[10] Ihsan blogs as Sir Cam, and photographing the mosque is one of his abiding passions.

The portico, with its huge, shady overhang, is a very good place to sit and talk – or, in the case of Ihsan, laugh a good deal as you talk.

WELCOME TO THE MOSQUE: A TOUR INTO THE HEART OF THE SACRED 123

(LEFT) Octagonal window and crenellations crowning the Prayer Hall external wall

(BELOW) External wall of the Prayer Hall showing low air vents and crenellations at the top

(OVERLEAF) Stone crenellations around the top of the prayer hall walls symbolising the meeting of heaven and earth

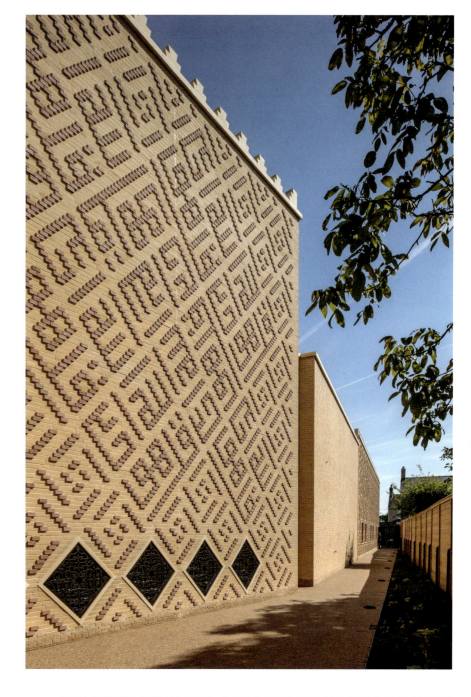

WELCOME TO THE MOSQUE: A TOUR INTO THE HEART OF THE SACRED

We are now beneath the first four of the mosque's symbolic trees, whose range of meanings encompasses the Tree of Life, rootedness, knowledge, that upward, open-handed movement from earth to sky. The fact that the four crab apple trees out in the garden are reflected in the great glazed doors through which we pass from the portico to the atrium seems to suggest that nature is being beckoned inside. In fact, this portico is both an outside and inside feature. There is a Qur'anic verse which translates as 'Say he is God, the One' (*sura* 112) partially concealed amongst the flurry of abstract patterning.

I mention to Ihsan that this was the first mosque that Marks Barfield Architects had ever created. Was it a success from his point of view? 'They have understood mosqueness, that is how I would put it. It is both like and unlike a mosque. It challenges the Muslim, I believe. It is both hi-tech and very simple, a wonderful fusion of elements, an interpretation if you like, a new freshness . . .' An exploration, I suggest, of the very meaning of the word mosque? Yes, he nods, 'According to the Qur'an a mosque is a prayer hall, a prayer chamber, the place where Mary prayed . . . For some this mosque is too bland and too minimalist. They want more colour, more decoration . . .' Fairly radical thinking has made this mosque what it is.

Yes, there is no minaret, and no call to prayer that you can hear out in the street. This mosque is an interpretation – like every new attempt to translate the Qur'an into English. Is there one version of the Qur'an that I would recommend

to you? Well, you might try Abdel Haleem's Oxford World's Classics version, or the one by Nuh Ha Mim Keller that I was sampling on YouTube only yesterday. Muslims are not a monolithic group. The Muslims of Cambridge are the representatives of about 70 different countries. The point is that the building should look outward, that it should not be regarded as a strange or an alien thing, something to be feared or mistrusted. So it is also, while being a place of prayer and prostration, a civic and a community building which reaches out in its very openness.

From the portico we enter the atrium, where our shoes come off. This is a meeting place which can also double as an auditorium, with seats for 200 people. Here conferences can be staged, weddings celebrated. The walls are once again of yellow gault brick, hanging from a timber framework, with coloured highlights in brown brick. The cross-hatching is very characteristic of the Victorian era, but the letters are Arabic, in blockish Kufic script, and once again we are reading the quotation from the Qu'ran: 'Say he is God, the One', the central message of Divine unity. Kufic is, according to Seyyed Hossein Nasr, 'the calligraphic style most closely associated with the Sacred Text, and the first in which the Word of God was written in Arabic'.[11]

Each quotation is square in formation. These squares are also circular in movement. They tilt. 'They are perfectly positioned, these bricks', Ihsan tells me. 'One swivel too far and the meaning would be lost. These ghostly

(OVERLEAF) Cambridge Central Mosque atrium on opening day

Qur'anic references are here to be deciphered by those who understand . . . And all made with such basic materials, and, as with so much else in this building, such sophistication: hi-tech, made to look very simple . . .'[12] The floor is covered in marble tiles, alternations of greys and whites, with a russet star at the centre of each octagon. The eight-pointed star dominates, and we see that it is replicated again and again as our eye sweeps across from front to back or from side to side. It is in the placing, and the interplay, of these tiles that you see very clearly visualised the meaning of 'the breath of the compassionate', Keith Critchlow's chosen geometric scheme for much of this building – how the octagon with a star at its centre seems to expand and contract, a metaphorical reference to how humans themselves breathe in and out.

We look back through the glazed doors, beyond the garden to the bus stop. The doors fit so well that now we can see the hurry of the teeming world outside, but barely hear it at all. It is visibly present, but also set apart from us. Silence seals us indoors. The room feels comfortably heated. 'You see how the bus stop can be seen through the glass of the portico, Michael. This is not about retreating into a shell. It is about openness, open spaces, which are part outside and part inside . . .' Ihsan gently taps my shoulder. 'It is not just these trees and the colour of these bricks which are reminiscent of the local', he remarks as we pass out of the atrium in the direction of the prayer hall. 'This fountain at the heart of the Islamic garden reminds me of the fountain in Trinity's Great Court, and the importance of mathematics to this building puts me in mind of the Mathematical Bridge at Queens' College.'

But before leaving the atrium we pass through double doors to the right, into the cafe. Anyone is welcome here, of all creeds or none, to study, to drink a cup of tea, water or juice – all provided free of charge. I remark on the welcoming generosity of this gesture to Imam Sejad Mekic when we meet for a conversation. 'The cafe is open to Muslims and non-Muslims alike', he tells me, 'to stay here as long as you wish. In the words of the great poet Rumi, "Come, Come whosoever you are".'[13] There are flowers in abundance everywhere – a wedding has recently been celebrated here, and the families have left many flowers behind for us all to enjoy. 'A Muslim', the imam continues, 'has a duty to share food, to feed a friend or a neighbour'. They had hoped to open a restaurant, but there were problems with VAT because of the mosque's charitable status. The cafe is a space both civic and sacred, a little of both. Conversations go on here. Young people are busy at work on their laptops. Two of the great timber trees make for a commanding presence. It is early afternoon now, and Cambridge Central Mosque being built on a north–south axis means that the warmth of the sun has penetrated the cafe, and we are enjoying the benefits of passive heating. Discussing architectural matters interlaced with matters of theology and jurisprudence over tea proves to be a very pleasurable experience.

(PREVIOUS) The atrium bathed in natural light

(LEFT) The atrium, looking towards the ablutions rooms and prayer hall, showing the stone floor with 'the Breath of the Compassionate' pattern

(OVERLEAF) Visitors to the Cambridge Central Mosque enjoying a guided tour

WELCOME TO THE MOSQUE: A TOUR INTO THE HEART OF THE SACRED

(OPPOSITE) The atrium laid out with chairs for a wedding

(BELOW) Shadows on the atrium floor

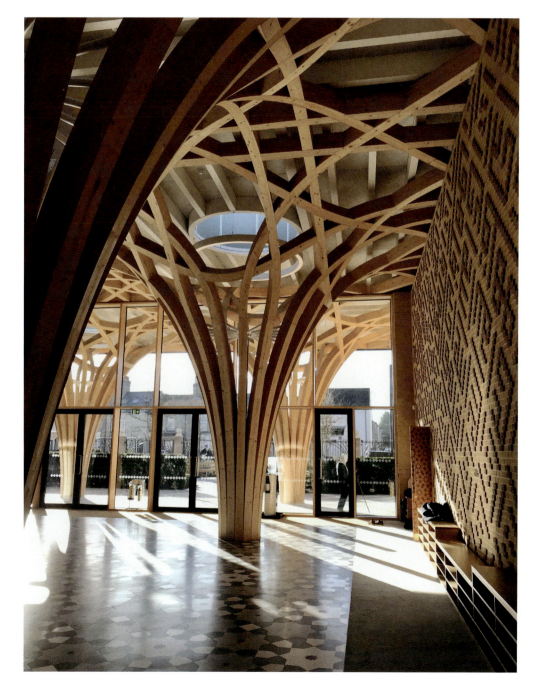

WELCOME TO THE MOSQUE: A TOUR INTO THE HEART OF THE SACRED   139

(OPPOSITE) View from the atrium looking towards the garden and Mill Road

(RIGHT) The imam showing a group of visitors around the mosque

(BELOW RIGHT) The brick Kufic pattern on the atrium walls reading 'Say he is God, the One', which is repeated with rotating symmetry

WELCOME TO THE MOSQUE: A TOUR INTO THE HEART OF THE SACRED   141

Portico brickwork

142 CAMBRIDGE CENTRAL MOSQUE

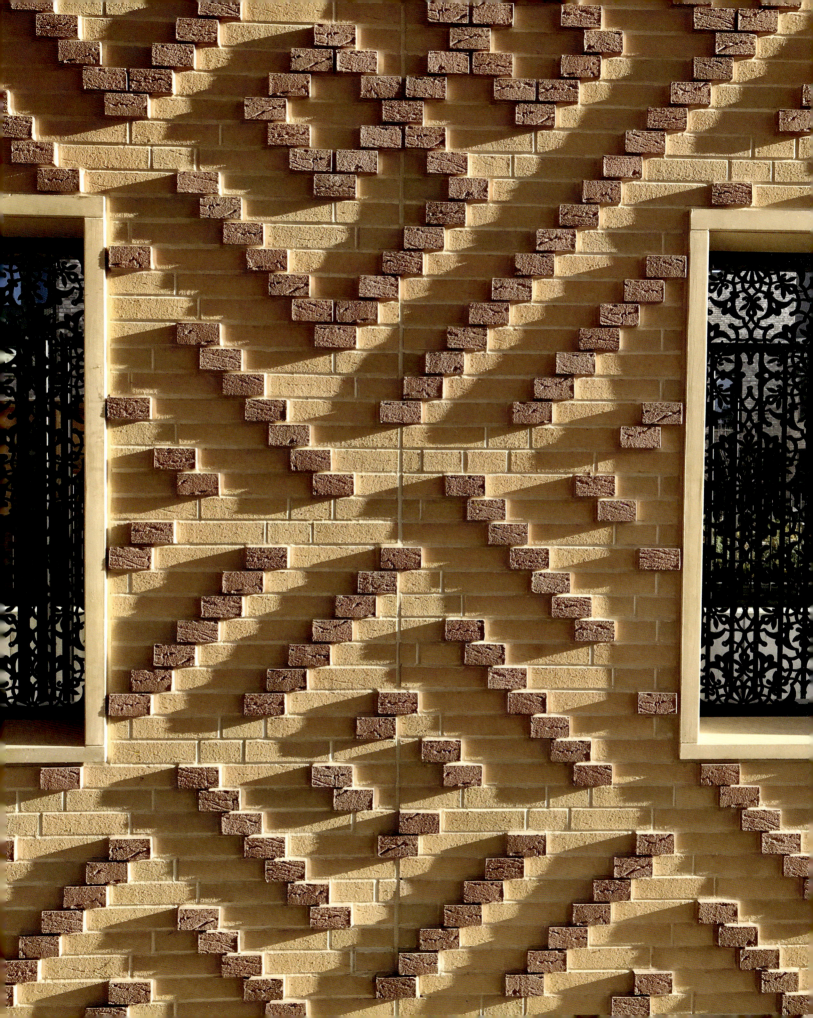

(LEFT) Male ablutions area with ample natural light and turquoise Spanish craquele tiles

(OPPOSITE) Octagonal female ablution area

Passing out of the cafe, we cross the atrium to the multi-purpose education room. The other day it was used for a wedding reception. It also doubles as an exhibition space which is currently showing a part-history of Islamic sciences, telling how the creation of ingenious scientific instruments helped Muslims to regulate and codify religious practices. The display cases are embedded into the walls, which leaves the floor entirely free so that other activities can go on in the room simultaneously.

Before we reach the prayer hall, we cross into what the architects describe as the 'knuckle' of the building. Above and below this space, out of sight, is the technology which controls much of the minimal energy use – heat pumps, etc. It is also from this interim space that we enter the ablution areas, females to the left, males to the right. 'Here we prepare to meet the Beloved', Ihsan remarks. Each of these two ablution areas – which come complete with foot driers and sensor-controlled taps – has natural skylights and dazzling turquoise tiles, made in Turkey and donated to the mosque by Çanakkale Ceramics. This is where various parts of the body are cleansed by a modest stream of preheated water (which is then harvested, filtered and reused to flush the toilets) in preparation for prayer: hands; face; arms up to the elbow; feet up to the ankles. The drain is very discreet – a channel accommodating a thin rivulet of water. Both rooms have a baby changing area.

The prayer hall, capacious enough to accommodate 1000 worshippers at prayer,

(OPPOSITE) Prayer hall and atrium threshold space

is this building's largest communal area, its innermost sanctum, and its best-kept secret – until we enter it, and experience, immediately, a feeling of awestruck amazement. It is angled differently from the rest of the building – the entire hall is skewed to the right (as if gently lifted and turned), at the behest of the geographical location of the Ka'ba in Mecca. When we stare at the procession of the grove of trees, we also experience a sudden jump of scale. These trees are much taller than the ones we have seen before, in the portico, cafe or atrium. It is as if nature has risen up to meet a greater and more august occasion. These trees 'symbolise the four imams of Sunni Islam and the twelve imams of Shia Islam, reflecting the spirit of unity which runs throughout the mosque', as we were informed in the booklet that accompanied the official opening in 2019.[14] The abundance of skylights, each one positioned above the top of its respective tree, makes for a constant play of natural light which can change from moment to moment – it entirely depends upon the whim of a scudding cloud. The fact that the skylights have this central position means that heat does not bear down on us, only light, and that light is itself dispersed – we see how shadows flow down the trunks of the trees in wave after wave of gentle, ghostly acts of light-painting.

The heat generated by so many during times of communal prayer is kept at a comfortable level in ways that we can't see. At floor level there are oak grilles, all designed by Keith Critchlow, beautified by marquetry, through which bodily heat is sucked up and out through air ducts. Fresh air comes in, and carbon dioxide is removed through the extractor fans (which are only activated when necessary). The design of the grilles is a play of arabesque – nature (trees and flowers) on the riot. If you look up at the skylights with care, you will see that beneath these 'oculi' – circular eyes of light – there are yet more grilles, resembling a kind of perforated circular wall through which heat is drawn out. Only when out on the roof of the prayer hall do you actually see the technology that makes this possible, the enclosing boxes that surround the oculi.

The prayer hall is a place of contemplative quiet, a zone in which you can disconnect from the headlong teem of the world, that 'calm oasis' promised by the architects, and somewhat reminiscent of the forest of palm trees which helped to define the Prophet's mosque in Medina. Ihsan and I watch the worshippers as they come and go – there are five official moments of prayer during the day, but worshippers are also free to come and go as and when they wish, there is no prohibition – and see how, having laid down their prayer rugs, they stand, one by one, and prepare themselves for the act of prayer, each in their own way, and at their own rhythm. Nothing is hurried.

He himself is Sunni Hanafi, Ihsan tells me. Shia and Sunni, he points out – all are equally welcome here; this is a non-denominational mosque – have different ways of holding their hands when they prepare to pray. Shia do not fold their hands when praying. He, on the other hand, holds his hands folded below the belly, or

The prayer hall

The prayer hall at peak prayer time on a typical Friday

(OPPOSITE) The dome, highlighting the three-dimensional pattern designed by Keith Critchlow based on a truncated cuboctahedron. This is one of the 13 Archimedean solids, which are semi-regular solids approximating a sphere using regular polygons.

150 CAMBRIDGE CENTRAL MOSQUE

WELCOME TO THE MOSQUE: A TOUR INTO THE HEART OF THE SACRED   153

(PREVIOUS LEFT) The prayer hall, with a solitary worshipper, bathed in natural light and showing the Turkish-made *mihrab* and *minbar*, with the *mashrabiya* screen to the rear separating the female prayer area

(PREVIOUS RIGHT) The prayer hall full of male worshippers, showing the *mihrab* and *minbar* and calligraphy

(BELOW) The prayer hall showing worshippers and the *mihrab* and *minbar*

(OPPOSITE) Stained glass window

154   CAMBRIDGE CENTRAL MOSQUE

(OPPOSITE) The imam leading prayers during the COVID-19 pandemic.

A woman photographing the prayer hall

WELCOME TO THE MOSQUE: A TOUR INTO THE HEART OF THE SACRED   157

– an equally acceptable variant – straight down. 'Prayer can be five minutes, five times a day', Ihsan tells me. 'Anyone can do it!'[15] All face the *mihrab* when praying.

Light illuminates the hall in ever-changing ways. One moment the room is relatively low-lit, and then, without warning, the light intensifies, and the colour of the wood deepens and becomes a nuttier brown. It is as if light is putting on display a show of its own miraculous mutability. There is no need for artificial lighting of any kind – the light from the sky, the light of the Divine presence made palpable here as a Muslim would express it, streaming down through one or another of the many skylights, does as much as needs to be done. We think, immediately, of Monet's great cycle of paintings of Rouen Cathedral made over a succession of days in the 1890s, and how changes of light throughout the progress of those days changed the appearance of the façade of that great cathedral. Reality itself seems to change even as you experience it. And so it is here, in this prayer hall.

The symbolic manifestation of the ceaseless, boundless creativity of nature does not begin and end with the upward movement of the trees, how they rise and then open out, as if both in support of the roof, and with a wish to travel further still. The fact is that there is no discernible end to yearning for the Divine, and so their spreading moves out across the ceiling above our heads in a kind of interweaving, intricate tracery of twisting beams – they resemble multiple arms which possess the kind of fluidity of movement to be seen in the Chola bronzes of Southern India, when Shiva dances for our delectation. And what happens when these beams reach the side walls? Do they merely stop? Not really. It looks to our eye as if they disappear into the walls, and then go on out into the world, still yearning to be in motion.

The prayer hall induces a mood of serenity that both calms the body and lifts the spirits. Its geometry and its symmetry remind us that we all crave some sense of order. Islam goes further, of course. It inserts the Divine into the equation. 'Art exists to remind us of what is just below the surface', Tim Winter explains to me in the cafe. 'Geometry and symmetry, those physical constants, the existence of order, are a calm reminder that the world itself is orderly, and under control. Otherwise, it would be pure anarchy . . .' And Marks Barfield's choice of a grove of trees, shown off to such splendid effect in the prayer hall, as the building's point of primary focus, is particularly apposite. 'Trees include us in nature, they enfold us', Tim comments. 'We feel at home when we are surrounded by it. Nature is a particular indicator of Divine agency. We reactivate our presence as God's agents . . .'[16]

The prayer hall is relatively unadorned in other respects. Around the walls, there are diamond-shaped recesses for accommodating copies of the Qur'an, but in Arabic alone – there is no such thing as a proper 'translation' of the Qur'an because Muslims believe their holy book to be untranslatable. There can only ever be books which generally describe

Marks Barfield Architects designed the *mashrabiya* screen at two heights, incorporating Keith Critchlow's patterns.

themselves as the 'meaning' of the Qur'an. Circular roundels set into the walls of the prayer hall contain Qur'anic quotations, in *thuluth* script (which dates from the 13th century). It is more rounded and curvy than the Kufic script to be seen in the brickwork. The colour of the carpet on the floor feels quite subdued and English in its combination of cool and relatively neutral colours – grey, with lines of magenta. Those lines help to indicate how one worshipper might keep their distance from another. 'Some worshippers find the hall more tonally subdued than expected', Ihsan tells me. 'They expect stronger colours. Such restraint surprises them.'[17]

The oak *mashrabiya* screen, a decorative lattice screen of delicately worked marquetry fabricated in Ulster, runs up the hall from north to south, dividing male from female worshippers in a way which does not feel severely prescriptive. Once again, as we recognise the repetition of the shape of the eight-pointed star, we think of the idea of 'the breath of the compassionate'. Julia Barfield feels especially proud to have been on the team of what is widely regarded as the most women-friendly mosque in the country. How to deal with the question of how women and men worship together in the prayer hall of a mosque? That was a key issue. Soundings were taken amongst the local community, and opinions were divided about the degree to which the sexes should be shielded from one another. The very first mosque had no screen at all. 'No barrier is legally necessary', Imam Sejad explains. 'The consensus was that both sides felt comfortable having something between.'[18]

The solution was an ingenious one. It was decided that the *mashrabiya* screen separating male from female worshippers should not only be of variable height, but also have a gap in the middle as if to emphasise the fact that both sexes are sharing the same prayer hall. Where you choose to stand, and to what degree you might or might not wish to be concealed, is a personal decision. You can pass through the gap if you wish. This screen is not fixed. One advantage of the mobile screen, Tim Winter comments when I mention it to him, is that it future-proofs the mosque against changes

WELCOME TO THE MOSQUE: A TOUR INTO THE HEART OF THE SACRED

(OPPOSITE TOP) Marks Barfield Architects designed the women's *mihrab*, incorporating Keith Critchlow's geometric pattern made in East London of patinated brass with polished high points.

(OPPOSITE BELOW) View of the women's *mihrab*

in the male–female ratio. It could even be removed altogether, should that ever be thought desirable in the future.[19]

'At first the screen was to have been 1.8 metres in height', Julia explains,

> but that was reduced in height, and in fact it is of variable height, higher at one end than the other. The point is that there is no absolute separation between men and women. They are all worshipping in the same prayer hall. What is more, there are three areas women can go to if they happen to feel uncomfortable in the main part of the mosque.[20]

There is a separate, soundproofed, prayer room for women and children next to the prayer hall on the ground floor, entered by glazed doors. This room contains its own women's *mihrab* set into the wall, a pared-back, simple, wooden structure, framed by turquoise enamelling, with threadings of brass to define the geometric patterning. 'This area exists to encourage women with young children to attend the mosque without feeling that their babies are disrupting the peace of the space', comments Tim Winter.[21] Passing through this room, you reach the staircase which takes you up to the Baraka Gallery, a balcony exclusively for the use of women, which is half-glazed, and therefore connected to the prayer hall which it overlooks. You can see it if you look up and to the left after entering the prayer hall. That balcony room was made possible by the

fundraising efforts of a remarkable young local woman called Baraka Khan. As a plaque on the gallery's back wall tells us, Baraka was diagnosed with lung cancer shortly after she graduated from Emmanuel College, Cambridge, in August 2013. Deeply devoted to her faith, and proud to be a British Muslim, she dedicated the energies of her final months to raising funds to pay for the completion of the mosque. She died at the age of 24 in 2016, having raised almost half a million pounds. 'It is a very young population of worshippers in general', Ihsan tells me as we look at the plaque, 'not all oldsters by any means'.[22] From this gallery you can look across the grove of 16 trees from a very high vantage point – you find yourself counting them to be quite sure there are so many. It feels as if you are sky-walking in nature.

Directly opposite, set into the far wall, you can see the *mihrab*, which is a recess, a niche set into the wall, which Ihsan describes as a very large prayer chamber, the place where the Prophet himself might once have stood. It is the principal focal point of the room. Narrow-arched and strikingly tall, its surround extends up to the height of the ceiling. 'The niche suggests the presence of the Prophet without in any way representing him', notes Keith Critchlow.[23] The roundels that flank the *mihrab* contain quotations from the opening *sura* of the Qur'an. The design of the *mihrab*, and the *minbar* which sits beside it (the pulpit from which the imam addresses worshippers), together with the roundels on the walls of the prayer hall displaying quotations from the

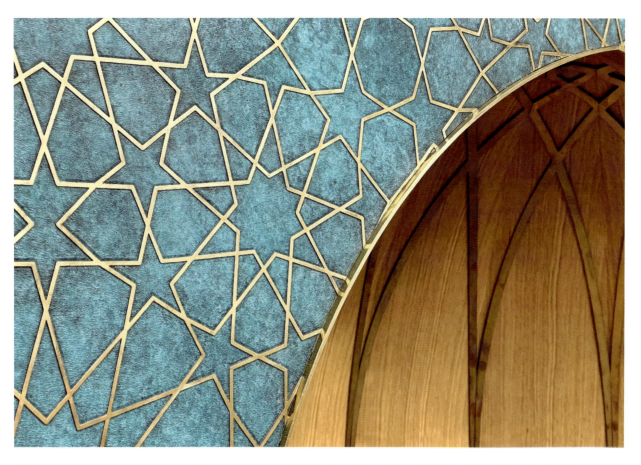

WELCOME TO THE MOSQUE: A TOUR INTO THE HEART OF THE SACRED 161

View of the women's areas to the rear of the prayer hall, with the mother and child area on the ground floor and the women's balcony above the Baraka Gallery

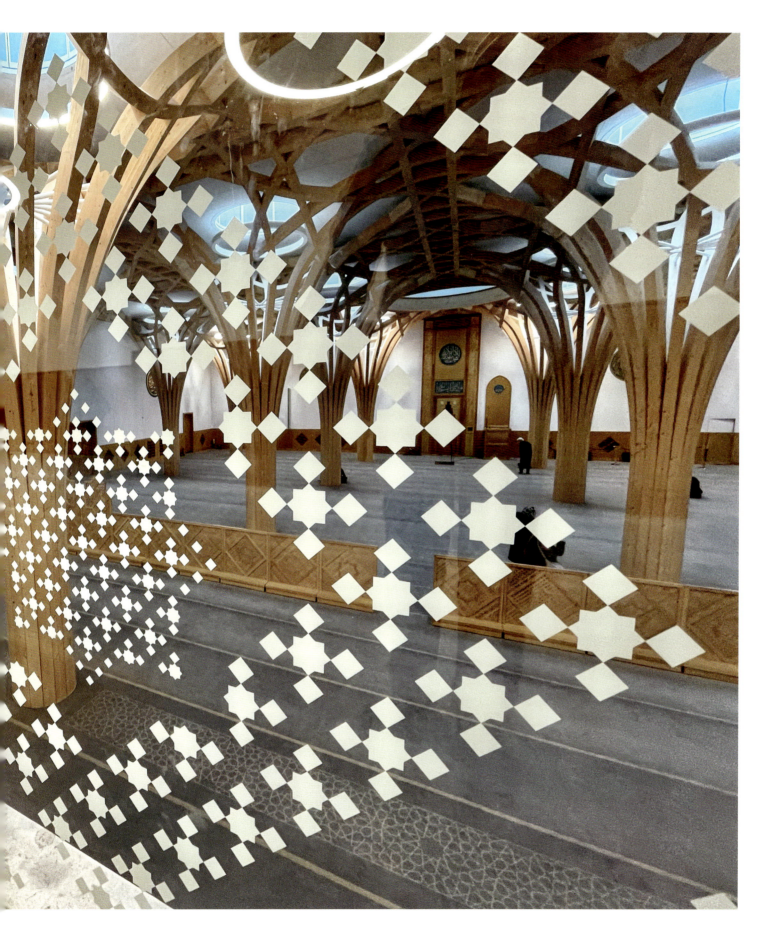

WELCOME TO THE MOSQUE: A TOUR INTO THE HEART OF THE SACRED 163

(LEFT) The first prayer on 15 March 2019, showing how the low *mashrabiya* screen, with a deliberate gap between the men's and women's areas, creates a more inclusive prayer space

(OPPOSITE) Keith Critchlow, sketch on top of dome section

Qu'ran, were all conceived in the Istanbul studio of Hüseyin Kutlu. On either side of the *mihrab*, set into the uprights which flank it, there are tiles in a recessed gold frame. These are Ottoman-era tiles from the Dome of the Rock in Jerusalem, that place of worship of such importance to three great religions, but a Muslim structure of particular significance to Islam because it is believed to be the place from which the Prophet of Islam ascended into Heaven. 'It was in Jerusalem', Tim Winter comments 'that the Prophet was said to have miraculously prayed with the souls of Jesus, Moses, Solomon and other prophets, underlining Islam's claim to affirm the entire line of Abrahamic revelation'.[24] These tiles were donated to the mosque by King Abdullah of Jordan. The building in Jerusalem was undergoing renovation and the old tiles were to be replaced by new ones. Now they are playing an important role in Cambridge Central Mosque, speaking of continuity and interdependency.

Directly opposite the wall containing the *mihrab*, raised up beyond the *mashrabiya* screen, you will see a fragment of cloth in a gold frame. This was a gift to the mosque from Ersin Arıoğlu, director of the Turkish engineering firm Yapı Merkezi, and it is a 19th-century fragment of the veil that covers the *Ka'ba* in Mecca, holiest of Muslim shrines. The cloth is renewed and replaced every year. These symbols from holy sites common to three great theistic religions face each other across the mosque.

It is only when you stand relatively close to the *mihrab* niche at the eastern end of the prayer hall that the small dome, a little offset to the side above your heads, really makes its presence felt. In Islamic tradition, the dome represents the vault of heaven. The dome in Cambridge Central Mosque is neither grand nor triumphal. In fact, its presence feels modest and delicate, as if it is making a reference to a feature common to many mosques around the world, but not in any way that is strident or attention-grabbing. There are stained glass windows, light blushings of blueness, around the base of its inner rim. It was fabricated in plywood, with plaster of Paris sections, Gemma

164   CAMBRIDGE CENTRAL MOSQUE

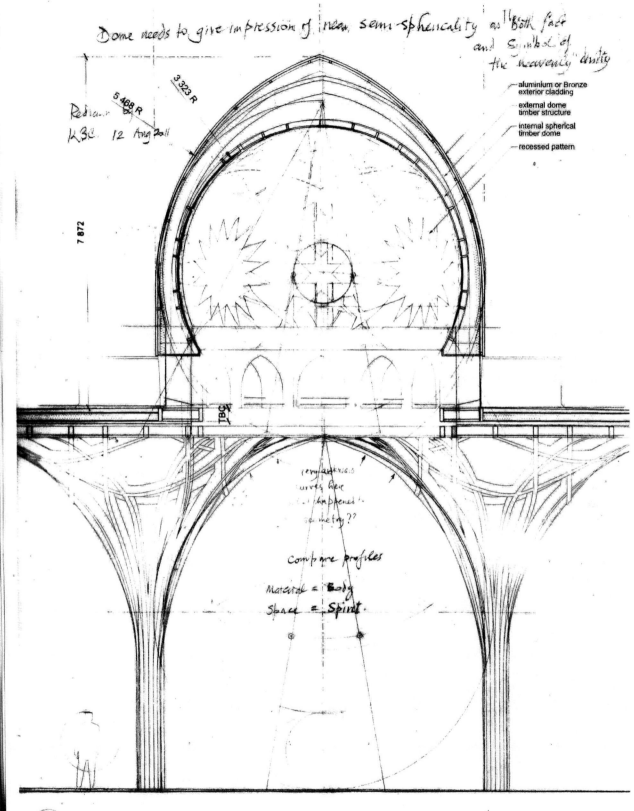

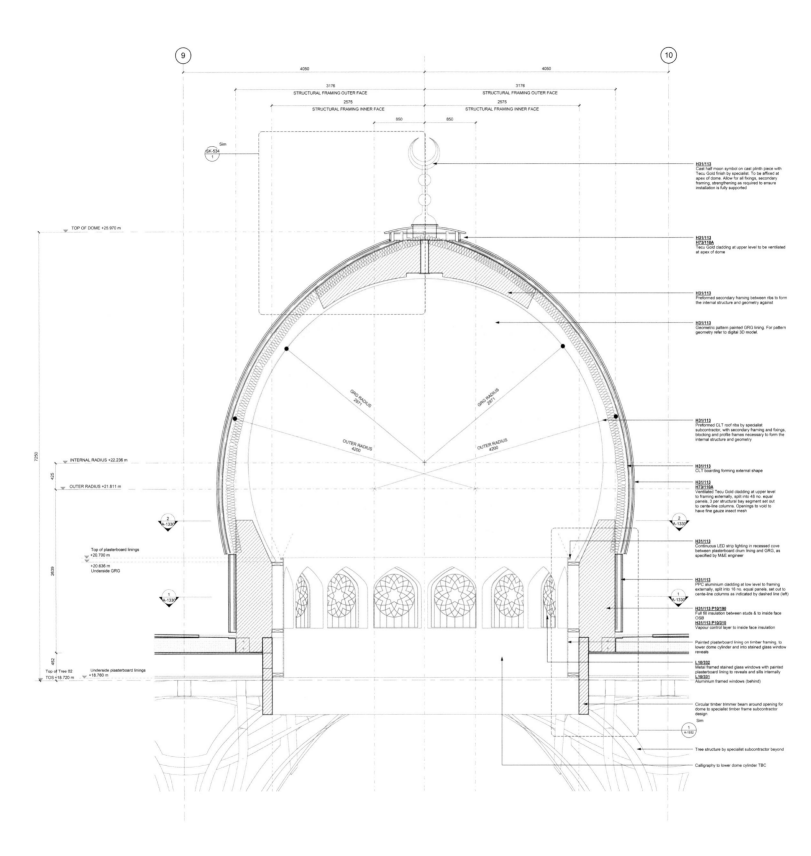

166   CAMBRIDGE CENTRAL MOSQUE

Marks Barfield Architects, dome section and dome 3-D section. It is not a requirement for a mosque to have a dome. However, domes do have significance in Islamic architecture and symbolise the vault of heaven. Celestial patterns and motifs are typically used to reflect this. The dome at Cambridge Central Mosque is offset towards the *qibla* wall on the central axis of the prayer hall.

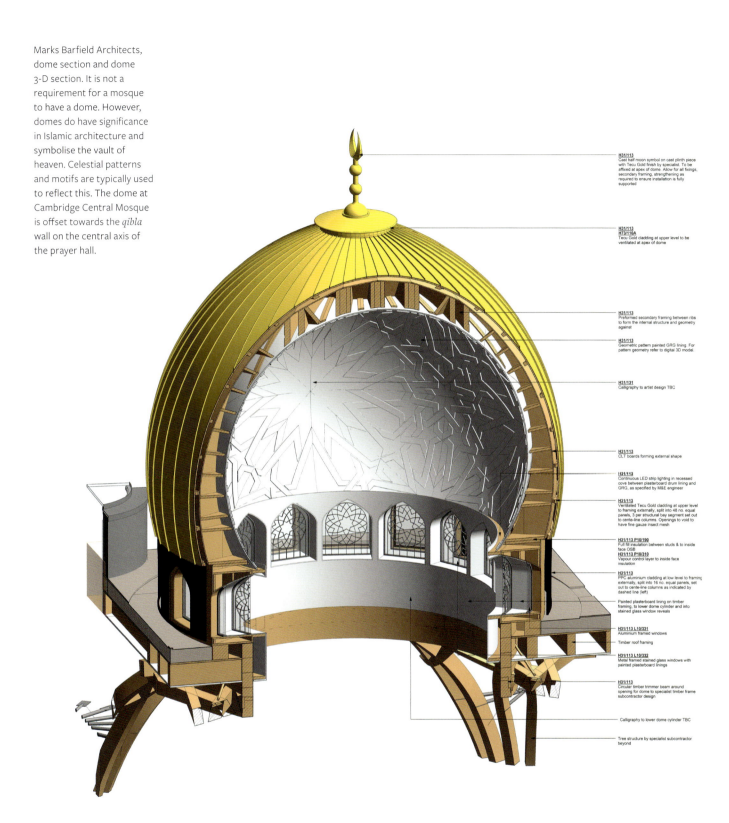

2 Dome 3D Section

WELCOME TO THE MOSQUE: A TOUR INTO THE HEART OF THE SACRED   167

(RIGHT) Keith Critchlow, sketch of the truncated cuboctahedron spherical grid with added 'flower + petals'. The truncated cuboctahedron is formed of regular hexagons, squares and octagons, reflecting the underlying building geometry. This geometry allows an expression of flowers with 8-, 12- and 16-fold petals.

(BELOW) Marks Barfield Architects, dome GRG panels, a geometrical panel breakdown for the dome

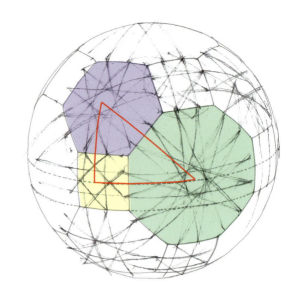

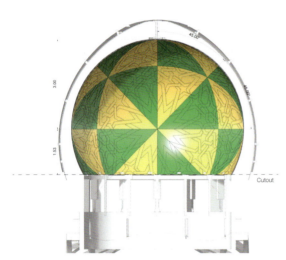

Dome GRG Surface Section

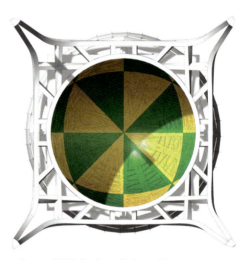

Dome GRG Surface Bottom View

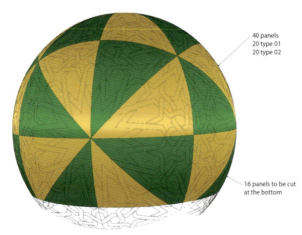

Dome GRG Surface

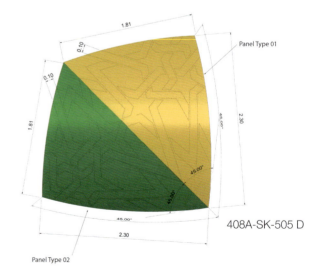

408A-SK-505 D

168 CAMBRIDGE CENTRAL MOSQUE

(BELOW) Fabrication of the dome panels

(BOTTOM) Panel prototype ready to form a mould

(OVERLEAF) Interior view of the dome with no artificial light

WELCOME TO THE MOSQUE: A TOUR INTO THE HEART OF THE SACRED

(LEFT) Bookcase in the prayer hall

(OPPOSITE) Exterior view of the dome in direct sunlight

(OVERLEAF) Metal decorative grill designed by Keith Critchlow

Collins explains to me.[25] The challenge lay in how to break up the different patterns and still end up with a single mould. Eventually the patterning was indicated by the most time-honoured and traditional of means: a swinging plumb line on the end of a string. The internal lining of the dome is lightly scored with a densely complicated scheme of geometric patterning based on a truncated cube octahedron (one of the 13 Archimedean solids), which is itself formed of regular hexagons, squares and octagons relating directly to the geometry of the building. The delicate scoring of the patterning, which unfolds like petals, feels almost ghostly in its lightness of touch. The dome's finial rises to 17 m in height.

From the upper roof of the prayer hall, you can stare across to the ever-growing presence of Addenbrooke's Hospital, and then out beyond to the flatlands of rural Cambridgeshire. This roof puts you on a level with the small golden dome, fabricated from painted plywood, which you can stare up and into when you stand close to the *qibla* wall and the *mihrab* in the prayer hall. If you look from the upper roof down towards the lower roof in the general direction of Mill Road and the south, you will see an array of photovoltaic panels. To the left, you will spot the green sedum roof, a moss-like succulent plant that does not need a lot of water. A sedum roof has various benefits: it helps with water attenuation, and it is particularly attractive to insects and butterflies. It also provides thermal insulation and contributes to biodiversity. 'The advantage of a sedum roof', Julia Barfield comments on the afternoon that we climb up a ladder onto the roof in order to get a clear view of what the hidden part of the building consists of, 'is that it can be thin and shallow'. Between the two main roofs there is the sunken roof of the building's 'knuckle', which is a service area. This deep-set channel in the middle of the building is of crucial importance to the successful working of this energy-efficient building – only from above can you see the snaking of fat air ducts, the noise pollution screen, the air-source heat pumps and much

172   CAMBRIDGE CENTRAL MOSQUE

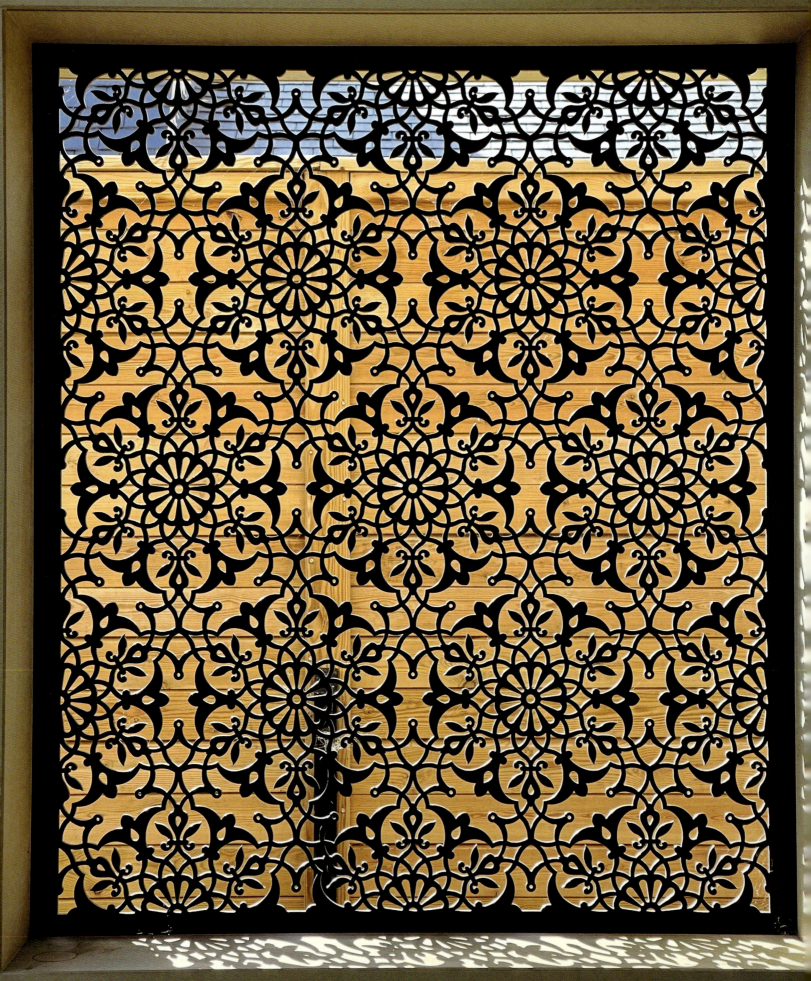

WELCOME TO THE MOSQUE: A TOUR INTO THE HEART OF THE SACRED

Detail of *mashrabiya* screen

Detail of the women's *mihrab* designed by Marks Barfield Architects in oak, brass strips and turquoise patinated brass with geometric relief pattern by Keith Critchlow

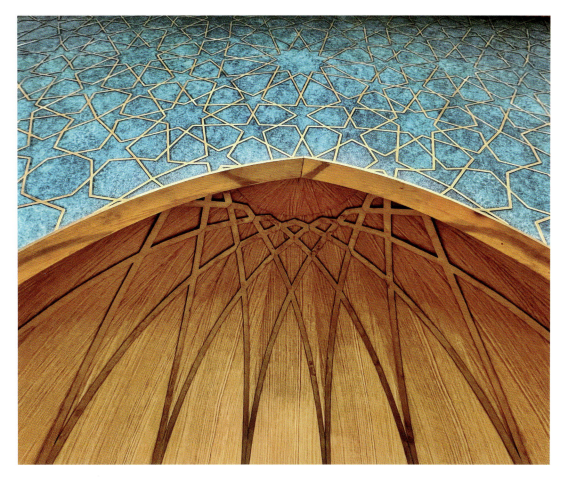

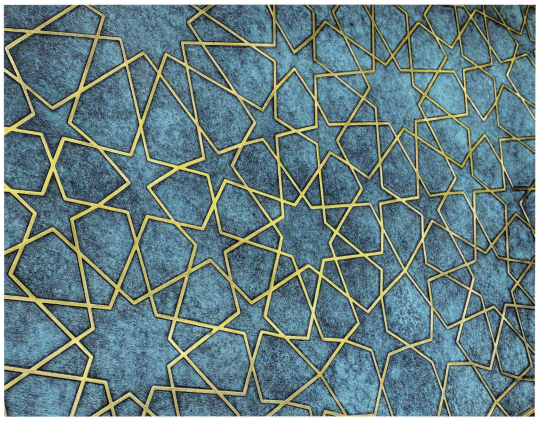

WELCOME TO THE MOSQUE: A TOUR INTO THE HEART OF THE SACRED 177

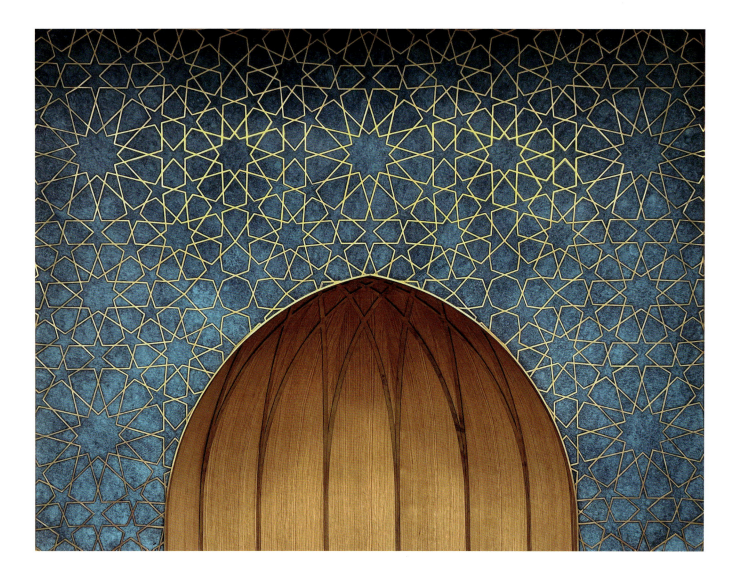

else. 'These are the concealed areas where all the hard work happens', Julia explains.[26]

Gemma Collins tries to summarise her experience of looking at and spending time at the mosque. 'What is so special', she tells me,

> is that it takes traditional materials and uses them in a contemporary way, a way that reflects technological advances. The whole building is a work of art. Yes, it is like walking through a work of art. It has such a calming presence. The sheer scale of the geometry, the height to which the trees rise, does bring such beauty to the space. The challenge lay in how to respect, appeal to, and respond to so many different traditions and cultures, people of different nationalities who were accustomed to different climates, those who grew up amongst different traditions of ecclesiastical architecture, to ensure they all felt included and could regard themselves as being a part of what we had made for them.[27]

(OPPOSITE) Door detail with bespoke pattern inlay designed by Keith Critchlow

178 CAMBRIDGE CENTRAL MOSQUE

ONE WEEK IN THE LIFE OF CAMBRIDGE CENTRAL MOSQUE

The social value of the mosque is to act as a unifying focus for the local Muslim community. A place of prayer, help, guidance, knowledge, advice, social intercourse. A place of pride of identity and remembrance of God. The physical values embodied in the mosque will express all the above in strength, beauty, and convenience, the materials expressing the most responsible attitude toward ecologically sound use and maintenance. It is intended to be a meeting place and a cultural bridge where modernity and innovation meet timeless sacred principles.[1]

KEITH CRITCHLOW

The Cambridge Central Mosque is both a civic and a spiritual centre. It looks inward insofar as it is a place of solace, spiritual nurture and teaching for the various Muslim communities of Cambridge and beyond. It also reaches out to the wider population, to those of other faiths or none, offering a message of welcome, and practical help of various kinds. Friday is of particular importance in the Muslim calendar, Imam Sejad Mekic explains as we sit talking in the cafe after early afternoon prayers are concluded.[2] 'The lives of many families revolve around this building. Friday is a special holiday, when the entire family comes to contemplate. On other days there are study circles, and, three times a week, children study at our madrassa. Local children learn Qur'anic memorisation. They are also taught the beginnings of an understanding of Classical Arabic.' The mosque reaches out to the wider academic community too. An interfaith conference in 2019, for example, the very first event in the new building, organised jointly with Cambridge Muslim College, the Protestant Theological Faculty in Tübingen and St Andrew's Biblical Theological Institute in Moscow, addressed the pressing issue of 'Green Theologies in Inter-religious Perspective'.

'During Ramadan of 2022 we had 20,000 people here, 1600 for early Friday prayers. In general, we have 2000 visitors a week, which means about 400 to 500 people per day, and about 1500 on Friday alone. All are welcome.' People are very curious as to what happens at a mosque, and how visiting a mosque differs from the experience of going to a church. How much formality is to be expected or required? We talk about the Great Mosque of Damascus, and of its openness to relaxed family gatherings. Cambridge Central Mosque feels that it has a civic duty to be as open to questioning as possible, in order that ignorance of Islam can be dispelled, and it can be seen as a transparent religion, with a relatively uncomplicated belief system (as he says those words, I think of the difficult doctrine of the Trinity); to remove from the faith any ingrained belief that it is essentially opposed to British values, or that it is to be mistrusted as an alien presence in our midst. I recall my conversation with the young imam at Shah Jahan Mosque in Woking, and how he had emphasised his belief in Jesus as a great prophet.

There is also too little knowledge, we agree, of what it is to visit a mosque, what the protocols are, what one might be expected to do or not to do, and whether it is even a desirable thing to be doing in the first place, especially if you are not a Muslim. There is of course the problem of belief and unbelief, and how that might affect one's behaviour. The poet Philip Larkin once captured this sense of

The café has become a real community hub, a place of social gatherings, work and study

puzzlement perfectly by describing the experience of visiting a Christian church as provoking a feeling of 'awkward reverence'.[3] Why awkward? And why reverence at all? How should we feel inside a mosque then? Cambridge Central Mosque is a building which feels neither prohibitive nor restrictive. Though sacred, it is also calmly and casually welcoming. It does not overbear or give off any fierce messages of Thou Shall Not. It seems to demand to be explored; to be waiting to be questioned in a reasonable way, in a spirit of mutual goodwill.

Since it opened in 2019, the mosque has garnered many architectural awards, and the story of its importance as a building has spread to every part of the world. Visitors come from all over: Japan, the US, Malaysia, all parts of Europe. It is a building which is both local and international, and a source of great pride to the Muslim community because someone, at last, has brought into being a building which seems worthy of their faith's significance and importance. Tours of the building are offered by volunteer tour guides (there are more than 10 such local guides at the time of writing), and these tours are always oversubscribed. On the day of a recent visit, a group from London was being led around the prayer hall by a guide called Alex Hetherington. This mosque is now part of his Cambridge itinerary of culturally and architecturally significant buildings, he tells me, along with King's College Chapel, the Bridge of Sighs at St John's College, the Mathematical Bridge at Queens' College and the Fitzwilliam Museum. How did the mosque come to be included in his itinerary? He talks about the 2021 RIBA award for the best new building in the East of England, and of the fact that the mosque was also shortlisted for the Stirling Prize in that same year. He is especially impressed by the awe-inspiring presence of the trees in the prayer hall, but also by the mosque's slow movement through from the noise and worldliness of the street, past the Islamic garden, and then finally on to this place of prayer and prostration. He looks up and seems to listen. The acoustics are astonishing, he says, but it is the trees which most engage him. 'I love the way the daylight plays on the

The café after Friday's prayers

ONE WEEK IN THE LIFE OF CAMBRIDGE CENTRAL MOSQUE

wood, enriching and deepening its tones.'[4] Visitors feel pleasingly marooned in a place where all clamour, hubbub and chaos seems to have been set aside.

The early afternoon call to prayer happens in front of the microphone, just a few feet away from the *mihrab* and the *minbar* in the prayer hall. It is inaudible from the street. The young man who makes the call has his hands pressed close against his ears as he cantillates the words. The call is broken into several parts, with significant pauses for the sound of his voice to resonate around the prayer hall before it dies away, and then resumes. As the call is being made, various worshippers walk in with their prayer mats. They lay them down, place their folded hands in front of their upright bodies, lean forward to an angle of 90 degrees, and then fully prostrate themselves. Each person attends to their own worship. Although the main element of the five daily prayers happens in unison, individual prayers of the kind we witness that afternoon are offered before and after. One or two are beginning to arrive even as others leave. Each act of singular worship seems to last about five minutes. After the call to prayer concludes, the director of the mosque walks over to the young man who has made it. They look at the microphone. They seem to be discussing voice projection. Meanwhile, worshippers are coming and going at their own pace, private devotion existing side by side with matter-of-fact, public conversation. This conjunction is very interesting to behold, a measure of informality in tandem with private acts of prayer. There are unspoken rules in place, too. There is no jocularity in the prayer hall, no babble of conversation. The conduct of visitors is uniformly quiet and respectful. It is as if how you experience the hall itself quietly dictates to the individual conscience how it would be appropriate to behave there.

Imam Sejad is the oldest of the three imams at the mosque, and he is from Bosnia. We are having a conversation about the role of the imam in a mosque such as this one.[5] His young colleague has also arrived to participate. Imam Sejad takes the lead, while Imam Zakarya Gangat, who comes from Canada and is also a personal trainer, spends much of the time listening seriously and intently as he stares down at his knees and gently rocks backwards and forwards. We talk about informality at the mosque, and the ways in which Islam differs from Christianity. There is no priestly hierarchy. No canons. No bishops. No curates. 'We are not superior to members of our congregation', he explains. Nor do they have a day off from their duties. The imam's living quarters are within the mosque itself, through a near-invisible door (white against the white wall) which leads off from the prayer hall, adjacent to the *minbar*. What qualifications are required of an imam? 'Memorisation of the Qur'an', he replies:

> The word imam means leader of the masses. Learning is of great importance. An imam must study jurisprudence and its application. We tell the back story of the occasion of

184   CAMBRIDGE CENTRAL MOSQUE

the Revelation to the Prophet. It is our task to share authentic knowledge, to explain the *hadiths*, that chain of narratives which accumulated after the Revelation itself, in order to give the correct attributions. An imam should also have knowledge of the Islamic sciences, and of the Classical Arabic language, but no human must be overburdened.

To each according to his gift and talents then – some were born to be orators, others not. There is clearly a reverence for scholarship. He who is most learned must be listened to. We talk a little more about the Great Mosque in Damascus, what a social space it is, how children play, while others sleep, and families eat and talk. 'There is some moral policing in larger mosques, where it is impossible to know what is happening in every part of the building. Self-governance is very important. It is a matter for the individual. Here there is no eating and drinking in the prayer hall.'

Unlike even the most important of Christian churches, the mosque also has a mortuary. 'Key stages in the cycle of life are acknowledged at the mosque', the imam explains.

We celebrate an arrival, and we also offer support, including funeral prayers, at the end of life. We wash the body, wrap it, and bury it in the ground. We help the bereaved family with food if that is needed. We offer follow-up events. We do not practise cremation. Is the earth not big enough to

bury a body? The Qur'an is strong on this. The only exception is when someone dies at sea.

When it is not serving the needs of the spirit, the mosque attends to the needs of the body in ways that are fluid and ever-changing. A whole-day Diabetes Education Day happened in Cambridge recently. Money is raised regularly for the Macmillan Cancer Support – cakes are baked and sold. There is a clothes bank on-site. Food packages are distributed to local refugee communities. The mosque served as a pop-up vaccination centre at the height of the pandemic. The cafe has tea, water and juice freely available on a long table beside the wall. 'We are here to provide. It is our duty', the imam reminds me, 'to share food, to feed a stranger as readily as one would a friend or neighbour'. The mosque continues to look outward, in a gesture of welcome.

Cambridge Urban Sketchers
at the mosque

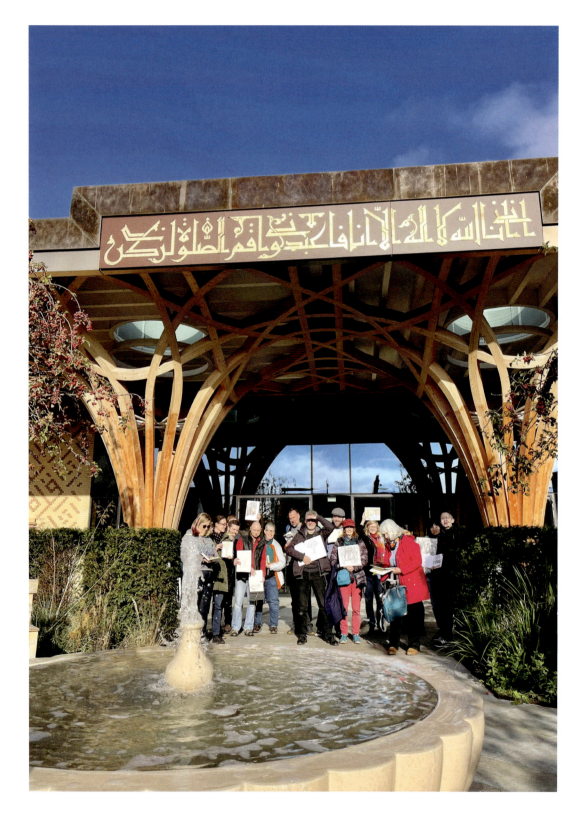

(TOP) Ibn Ali Miller at Cambridge Central Mosque, 18 February 2020

(MIDDLE) Eid-al-Fitr prayers at Cambridge Central Mosque led by Tim Winter (Sheikh Abdul-Hakim Murad)

(BOTTOM) The local Chief Constable Nick Dean visiting Cambridge Central Mosque and being shown around by the community

ONE WEEK IN THE LIFE OF CAMBRIDGE CENTRAL MOSQUE 187

(LEFT) Islamic science exhibition being enjoyed by visitors

(OPPOSITE) The teaching/exhibition space is multi-use, for seminars, lectures, weddings and more. It also displays a permanent exhibition of Islamic science

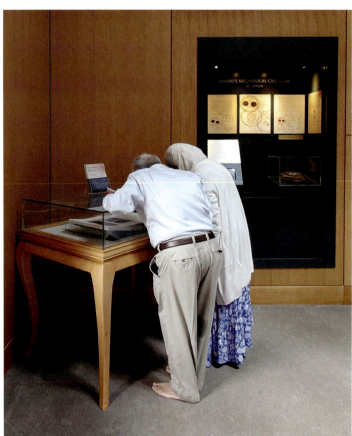

(LEFT) A couple studying one of the displays

(BELOW LEFT) Tim Winter (Sheikh Abdul-Hakim Murad) in the atrium

(BELOW RIGHT) London to Cambridge bikers reach Cambridge Central Mosque

(OPPOSITE) The groom meets guests in a traditional wedding at Cambridge Central Mosque

190 CAMBRIDGE CENTRAL MOSQUE

(OPPOSITE) Guests at a wedding

(RIGHT) Tim Winter (Sheikh Abdul-Hakim Murad) giving a tour at the mosque

(BELOW) A mother and child in the atrium of the Cambridge Central Mosque

Mosque volunteers serving refreshments to visitors and NHS staff doing health check-ups at Cambridge Central Mosque

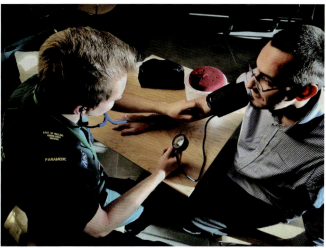

ONE WEEK IN THE LIFE OF CAMBRIDGE CENTRAL MOSQUE 195

(BELOW) Mortuary facilities at the Mosque

(OPPOSITE) Front door to one of the two on-site residencies

196   CAMBRIDGE CENTRAL MOSQUE

Women and children in the prayer hall

(OPPOSITE) A child in the atrium

198   CAMBRIDGE CENTRAL MOSQUE

ONE WEEK IN THE LIFE OF CAMBRIDGE CENTRAL MOSQUE 199

NOTES

INTRODUCTION

1 'Official Opening Ceremony of the Cambridge Central Mosque', booklet, 5 December 2019.

WHAT IS A MOSQUE?

1 Shahed Saleem, *The British Mosque: An architectural and social history* (Historic England: Swindon, 2018), p.3.

2 *Hadith* 1057:4; see https://hadithcollection.com/sahihmuslim/sahih-muslim-book-04-prayer/sahih-muslim-book-004-hadith-number-1057.

3 This remark and others quoted were made in the course of a conversation with Sejad Mekic at Cambridge Central Mosque on 9 May 2022.

4 Quoted in Lex Hixon (Nur al-Jerrahi), *Atom from the Sun of Knowledge* (PIR Publications: Westport, CT, 1993), p.147.

5 Saleem, *The British Mosque*, p.10.

6 ibid.

7 ibid., p.18.

8 Quoted in a text panel at the Woking Museum; see I. Nairn and N. Pevsner, *The Buildings of England: Surrey*, 2nd edn (Penguin Books: London, 1982), pp 533–4.

9 Conversation with Khalil Mohammed outside the Shah Jahan Mosque in Woking, 8 June 2022.

10 *Cambridge Evening News*, 2001.

11 Statistics about the Muslims of Cambridge courtesy Dr Chris Moses, personal communication, August 2018.

12 This remark and others quoted were made in the course of a conversation with Tim Winter at Cambridge Central Mosque on 10 May 2022.

13 David Marks, Cambridge Forum for the Construction Industry (CFCI) presentation, February 2017, text to accompany slide 13, held in the archives of Marks Barfield Architects.

14 This remark was made in the course of a conversation with Ian Rudolph at the offices of Marks Barfield Architects in Clapham, south London, on 29 June 2022.

15 Jonathan Glancey, 'The ideal dome show', *The Guardian*, 17 June 2002.

16 Conversation with Tim Winter, Cambridge Central Mosque, 10 May 2022.

17 This remark was made in the course of a conversation at the home of Julia Barfield in Clapham on 28 April 2022.

18 Conversation with Julia Barfield, 28 April 2022.

19 Marks Barfield Architects, public art delivery plan, 4 November 2011, held in the archives of Marks Barfield Architects.

20 David Marks, Cambridge Forum for the Construction Industry (CFCI) presentation, February 2017, text to accompany slide 22, held in the archives of Marks Barfield Architects.

21 Conversation with Ian Rudolph, Marks Barfield Architects, 29 June 2022.

22 Saleem, *The British Mosque*, p.231.

JULIA BARFIELD AND DAVID MARKS: PRACTISING THE ART OF IDEALISM

1 Conversation with Julia Barfield at her home in Clapham on 28 April 2022.

2 Marks Barfield Architects, *Gentle Landmarks* (Watermark Publications: Haslemere, Surrey, 2010), is an excellent account of their major projects during the decade after the completion of the London Eye, and my account draws on this book.

3 Quotes taken from a conversation with Julia Barfield at her home in Clapham on 28 April 2022.

KEITH CRITCHLOW AND THE SACRED ART OF GEOMETRY

1 Buckminster Fuller, quote used on the cover of Keith Critchlow, *Order in Space: A Design Source Book* (Thames & Hudson: London, 1969).

2 Keith Critchlow, 'Mosque Focus', note written in July 2009, held in the archives of Marks Barfield Architects.

3 Plato, *The Republic*, trans. Paul Shorey, in *Plato in*

Twelve Volumes, Loeb Classical Library, vols 5–6 (Harvard University Press and William Heinemann Ltd: Cambridge, MA, and London, 1969–70), vol.6, Book 7, p.527.

4 David Marks, note, 2008, held in the archives of Marks Barfield Architects.

5 Keith Critchlow, note written in 2017, held in the archives of Marks Barfield Architects.

6 Critchlow, 'Mosque Focus'.

7 Keith Critchlow, *Islamic Patterns: An Analytical and Cosmological Approach* (Thames & Hudson: London, 1976), p.57.

8 Shahed Saleem, *The British Mosque: An Architectural and Social History* (Historic England: Swindon, 2018), p.8.

9 David Marks, Cambridge Forum for the Construction Industry (CFCI) presentation, February 2017, text to accompany slide 62, held in the archives of Marks Barfield Architects.

10 Conversation with Ian Rudolph at the offices of Marks Barfield Architects in Clapham, south London, on 29 June 2022.

11 Conversation with Tim Winter, Cambridge Central Mosque, 10 May 2022.

12 Critchlow, 'Mosque Focus'.

13 This remark and others quoted were made in the course of a conversation with Guilherme Ressel at the offices of Marks Barfield Architects in Clapham, south London, on 3 May 2022.

THE TREES! THE TREES!

1 This conversation with Shahida Rahman took place at Cambridge Central Mosque on 9 May 2022.

2 Conversation with Julia Barfield at her home in Clapham on 28 April 2022.

3 This conversation with Jephtha Schaffner took place at the offices of Marks Barfield Architects in Clapham on 23 May 2022.

4 Conversation with Tim Winter, Cambridge Central Mosque, 10 May 2022.

SUSTAINABILITY

1 Conversation with Tim Winter, Cambridge Central Mosque, 10 May 2022.

2 This conversation with Matthew Wingrove took place at the offices of Marks Barfield Architects in Clapham, south London, on 22 April 2022.

3 David Marks, note, held in the archives of Marks Barfield Architects.

4 This conversation with Mark Maidment took place over Zoom on 12 May 2022.

5 This conversation with Julia Barfield took place at Cambridge Central Mosque on 11 May 2022.

6 Conversation with Matthew Wingrove, project architect, at the offices of Marks Barfield Architects in Clapham, 22 April 2022.

WELCOME TO THE MOSQUE: A TOUR INTO THE HEART OF THE SACRED

1 This brief roadside conversation with Sayedur Rahman took place outside Cambridge Central Mosque on the morning of 9 May 2022.

2 This conversation with Gemma Collins took place over coffee at Portcullis House, Westminster, on the afternoon of 27 May 2022.

3 David Marks, note, 2009, held in the archives of Marks Barfield Architects.

4 Diana Darke, *Stealing from the Saracens: How Islamic Architecture Shaped Europe* (Hurst & Co.: London, 2020), pp 183–4.

5 According to a BBC news report of 16 February 2016, it was in 1984 that the then Prince Charles described the proposed new extension to the National Gallery in this way. The extension, suitably modified, eventually became known as the Sainsbury Wing.

6 David Marks, note, 2009, held in the archives of Marks Barfield Architects.

7 This conversation with Emma Clark took place on the mezzanine floor of the British Library on 31 May 2022. See also Emma Clark, *The Art of the Islamic Garden* (The Crowood Press: Ramsbury, Wiltshire, 2004).

8   This conversation with Helen Seal took place in the garden of Cambridge Central Mosque on 9 May 2022.

9   Conversation with Emma Clark, British Library, 31 May 2022.

10 This conversation with Ihsan took place as he led me on a tour through Cambridge Central Mosque on the morning of 9 May 2022.

11 Seyyed Hossein Nasr, *Islamic Art and Spirituality* (State University of New York Press: Albany, NY, 1987), p.30.

12 Conversation with Ihsan, Cambridge Central Mosque, 9 May 2022.

13 This conversation with Imam Sejad Mekic took place in the cafe of Cambridge Central Mosque on 10 May 2022. For the full, translated text of this poem by Jelaluddin Rumi (1207–73), go to https://www. goodreads.com/quotes/79822.

14 'Official Opening Ceremony of the Cambridge Central Mosque', booklet, 5 December 2019.

15 Conversation with Ihsan, Cambridge Central Mosque, 9 May 2022.

16 Conversation with Tim Winter, Cambridge Central Mosque, 10 May 2022.

17 Conversation with Ihsan, Cambridge Central Mosque, 9 May 2022.

18 Conversation with Sejad Mekic, Cambridge Central Mosque, 10 May 2022.

19 Conversation with Tim Winter, Cambridge Central Mosque, 10 May 2022.

20 Conversation with Julia Barfield at her home in Clapham on 28 April 2022.

21 Conversation with Tim Winter, Cambridge Central Mosque, 10 May 2022.

22 Conversation with Ihsan, Cambridge Central Mosque, 9 May 2022.

23 Keith Critchlow, 'Mosque Focus', note written in July 2009, held in the archives of Marks Barfield Architects.

24 Conversation with Tim Winter, Cambridge Central Mosque, 10 May 2022.

25 Conversation with Gemma Collins, Portcullis House, Westminster, 27 May 2022.

26 Conversation with Julia Barfield, Cambridge Central Mosque, 11 May 2022.

27 Conversation with Gemma Collins, Portcullis House, Westminster, 27 May 2022.

ONE WEEK IN THE LIFE OF CAMBRIDGE CENTRAL MOSQUE

1   Keith Critchlow, 'Mosque – Divine Presences', note written in July 2009, held in the archives of Marks Barfield Architects.

2   Conversation with Sejad Mekic, Cambridge Central Mosque, 10 May 2022.

3   Philip Larkin, 'Church Going' (1955), l.9.

4   This conversation with Alex Hetherington took place at Cambridge Central Mosque on 10 May 2022.

5   This conversation with Imam Sejad Mekic and Imam Zakarya Gangat took place in the cafe of Cambridge Central Mosque on 10 May 2022.

BIBLIOGRAPHY

Ali, Abdullah Yusuf, trans., *The Holy Qur'an* (Wordsworth Editions: Ware, Herefordshire 2000).

Anderson, J.N.D., ed., *The World's Religions* (Inter-Varsity Fellowship: London, 1950).

Arberry, Arthur J., *The Koran Interpreted* (Oxford University Press: Oxford and New York, 2008).

Ardalan, Nader, and Laleh Bakhtiar, *The Sense of Unity: The Sufi Tradition in Persian Architecture* (University of Chicago Press: Chicago, IL, 1973).

Bloom, Jonathan M., *Architecture of the Islamic West: North Africa and the Iberian Peninsula* (Yale University Press: New Haven, CT, 2020).

Burckhardt, Titus, *Art of Islam: Language and Meaning*, commemorative edn (World Wisdom: Bloomington, IN, 2009).

Clark, Emma, *The Art of the Islamic Garden* (The Crowood Press: Ramsbury, Wiltshire, 2004).

Cleary, Thomas, *The Essential Koran* (HarperCollins: New York, 1993).

Cole, Peter, trans. and ed., *The Dream of the Poem: Hebrew Poetry from Muslim and Christian Spain 950–1492* (Princeton University Press: Princeton, NJ, 2007).

Critchlow, Keith, *Order in Space: A Design Source Book* (Thames & Hudson: London, 1969).

—, *Islamic Patterns: An Analytical and Cosmological Approach* (Thames & Hudson: London, 1976).

—, *The Hidden Geometry of Flowers: Living Rhythms, Form and Number* (Floris Books: Edinburgh, 2014).

Darke, Diana, *Stealing from the Saracens: How Islamic Architecture Shaped Europe* (Hurst & Co.: London, 2020).

Dawood, N.J., trans. and notes, *The Koran* (Penguin: Harmondsworth, 1956).

Frishman, Martin, and Hasan-Uddin Khan, eds, *The Mosque: History, Architectural Development and Regional Diversity* (Thames & Hudson, London, 1994).

Hixon, Lex (Nur al-Jerrahi), *Atom from the Sun of Knowledge* (PIR Publications: Westport, CT, 1993).

Mahmutćehajić, Rusmir, *The Mosque: The Heart of Submission* (Fordham University Press: New York, 2006).

Marks Barfield Architects, *Gentle Landmarks* (Watermark Publications: Haslemere, Surrey, 2010).

Moustafa, Ahmed, *The Attributes of Divine Perfection: The Concept of God in Islam* (Fe-Noon Ahmed Moustafa: London, 2007).

Murata, Sachiko, and William C. Chittick, *The Vision of Islam* (Paragon House: London and New York, 1994).

Nasr, Seyyed Hossein, *Islamic Art and Spirituality* (State University of New York Press: Albany, NY, 1987).

Pickthall, Marmaduke, *The Meaning of the Glorious Koran* (A.A. Knopf: New York, 1930).

Rose, Steve, and Marcus Robinson, *Eye: The Story behind the London Eye* (Black Dog: London, 2007).

Saheeh International, *The Meanings of the Qur'an in English* (Dar Qiraat: Riyadh, 2011).

Saleem, Shahed, *The British Mosque: An Architectural and Social History* (Historic England: Swindon, 2018).

Smith, Huston, *The Religions of Man* (Harper: New York, 1958).

Wilson, Eva, *Islamic Designs for Artists and Craftspeople* (Dover Publications: London, 1988).

DESIGN AND CONSTRUCTION TEAM

MARKS BARFIELD ARCHITECTS

David Marks, Julia Barfield, Gemma Collins, Matthew Wingrove, Brenda Kim, Guilherme Ressel, Ian Rudolph, Ian Crockford, Jolien Bruin, Amy Gaspar-Slayford, Liam Croft, Jonathan Kirby, Samuael Lyons, Urzula Markiewicz, Heena Mistry, Mustacha Musa, Wojciech Omiljanowski, Yushi Zhang, and environmental engineer, Loren Butt.

DESIGN

Client: The Cambridge Mosque Trust
Architect: Marks Barfield Architects
Project manager: Bidwells
Planning consultant: Bidwells
Structural engineers:
- David Tasker, Ramboll (competition stage)
- Jacobs (planning)
- Price & Myers (construction)

Building services engineer: Skelly & Couch
Cost consultant:
- Quantem (competition)
- Gardiner & Theobald (planning)
- Faithful+Gould (construction)

Mass timber engineer: Blumer Lehmann
Geometric artist: Professor Keith Critchlow with Islamic calligrapher Soraya Syed, Art of the Pen
Islamic Garden Designer: Emma Clark
Landscape Design: Urquhart & Hunt
CDM principal designer: Faithful+Gould
Timber consultant: Smith and Wallwork engineers
Acoustic consultant: Ramboll
Fire consultant: Harris TPS
Approved inspector: MLM, now Sweco

CONTRACTORS AND SUPPLIERS

Main contractor: Gilbert-Ash
Timber specialist: Blumer Lehmann
Brick tile cladding: Clarke Facades
Building services: Munro Building Services
Rooflights: Roofglaze
Bespoke joinery, doors and pannelling: The Deluxe Group
Dome internal lining: Blenheim Fine Interiors
Dome cladding: Exterior Metal Craft
Cast stone: Cunningham Stone
Tiling: Stonefit Ltd
Soft floor finishes: Floorform
Metalwork: Fleck Metal Solutions
Windows, fascias and cladding: Creative Aluminium Solutions
Curtain wall / glazed façade: Pacegrade
In-situ concrete: Fox Contracts
Precast concrete stairs: Acheson & Glover, now AG Professional
Piling: Keller
Roofing: The Green Roof Company
Balustrades & handrails: Laidlaw
Glazed internal doors: Planet Partitions
Railings and fencing: Jacksons Fencing
Soft landscaping: Landshaped
Fountain: Studio Ewing
Female *mihrab*: Capisco
Lighting: Spectral
Bespoke cast stone: Haddonstone
Photovoltaics: Silicon CPV
Tiling:
- Kale (ceramics)
- Intermarmor (marble)
- Domus (craquele glaze)

Curtain wall / glazed façade: Raico

Dome cladding: KME Tecu Gold
Carpet: Ege
Ironmongery: d line
Cubicles: Thrislington
Natural Stone Fountain: S McConnell & Sons
Coriam Brick Cladding: supplied by Taylor
    Maxwell and manufactured by Weinerberger

190 Members of the Marks Barfield Architects team who worked most extensively on the Cambridge Central Mosque project. Left to right, top to bottom: Brenda Kim, Gemma Collins, Guilherme Ressel, Heena Mistry, Ian Crockford, Ian Rudolph, Matthew Wingrove, Loren Butt, Wojciech Omiljanowski

DESIGN AND CONSTRUCTION TEAM   205

GLOSSARY OF SOME KEY ISLAMIC TERMS

TIMELINE

DHIKR devotional acts of remembering God

EID celebratory prayers at the end of Ramadan

HADITH commentary on the Qur'an

KA'BA 'the Cube', located in Mecca, built by Adam and rebuilt by Abraham, most holy of all Muslim sites, the point where the heavenly axis pierces the earth, and at the centre of the world

MASHRABIYA a latticed screen used as a room divider

MASJID mosque

MIHRAB prayer niche

MINBAR series of steps serving as a pulpit

QIBLA the direction of the Ka'ba

SURA chapter of the Qur'an

2006	Inception
2008	Purchase of site
February 2009	Competition announced
June 2009	Winning architect announced
7 September 2011	Local consultation
2011	Contact with Blumer Lehmann
22 August 2012	Planning application for the project unanimously approved
5 September 2016	Construction start date
11 October 2016	Groundbreaking ceremony
September 2017	Assembly of timber structure
30 November 2017	Topping out ceremony
February 2018	Completion of timber structure
15 March 2019	First prayer and welcoming event
April 2019	Soft opening

IMAGE CREDITS

Numbers refer to pages. 't', 'm', 'b', 'l', 'r' refer to 'top', 'middle', 'bottom', 'left', 'right' respectively.

Alamy Stock photo: 28, 96; Nader Ardalan and Laleh Bakhtiar, The Sense of Unity: The Sufi Tradition in Persian Architecture (University of Chicago Press: Chicago, IL, 1973): 70; Art Directors and TRIP / Alamy Stock photo: 19; Nic Bailey: 33; Julia Barfield: 199; Blumer Lehman: 72, 73, 74, 75t, 75b, 76, 77t, 77b, 78t, 78b, 79t, 79m, 79b, 80, 81t, 81b, 82t, 82b; Keith Critchlow: 43t, 43b, 46–47; Peter Durant: 32; Gary Eastwood: 9t; John Fielding: 38; Amelia Hallsworth: 64–65, 155, 159, 161t, 161b, 162; Julia C Johnson: 164, 191b, 193b, 198; Kevin Meredith: 36t; B.O'Kane / Alamy Stock photo: 99b; Paul Raftery: 36b; Marcus Robinson: 34–35; Marks Barfield Architects: 42, 44, 48, 49, 51, 52t, 52b, 53t, 66t, 67, 68, 69, 86t, 86b, 94t, 95, 98, 99t, 101, 102, 103, 104, 165, 166, 167, 168, 169; Guilherme Ressel: 123, 182, 183, 188t, 188b, 189, 196, 197; Sir Cam: 12, 14, 26, 27, 59, 60, 61, 83, 100, 105b, 106, 107, 108, 109, 110, 111, 112, 113, 114, 115, 116l, 116r, 117, 118t, 118b, 119, 120–121, 126–127, 137b, 138, 139, 140, 141t, 141b, 142, 143, 151, 152, 153, 154, 156, 157, 163, 170–171, 172, 173, 174, 175, 176, 177t, 177b, 178, 179, 186, 187t, 187m, 187b, 190l, 190r, 191, 192, 135, 193t, 194t, 194b, 195tl, 195tr, 195b; Jephtha Schaffner: 124; Skelly & Couch: 87t, 87b, 89t, 89b, 90; Morley von Sternberg: 39, 105t, 125, 132–133, 134, 136–137, 144, 145, 148–149, 150; Bill Taylor, Development and Coordination Director at Brockwood Park School: 10; Matthew Wingrove: 54-55, 56-57, 58, 146; Jan Wlodarczyk / Alamy Stock photo: 71; Nick Wood: 53b, 94b

INDEX

References to illustrations are set in *italics*.
All places are in Cambridge unless otherwise
stated.

ablution areas 88, 144, *144–5*, 147
Abu Bakr Islamic Centre 21–2, *22*
Arıoğlu, Ersin 164
atrium 128–9, *132–41*, 144, *193*, *199*

Baraka Gallery 160, *162*
Barfield, Julia *9*, 25–6, 31–8, 41, 70–1, 88, 159, 160, 172, 178
Blumer Lehmann 49, 70–80, *74–7*, 86
bookcases 21, *172*
Breath of the Compassionate (star pattern) 43–8, 82, 129
brickwork 98, *98*, 100, *142–3*
Brighton i360 *36*
Brighton Pavilion 19–20, 21
Butt, Loren 88

café 17, 129, *182–3*, 185
calligraphy 97, *98–9*, 128, *154*, 159
Cambridge University Real Tennis Club *100*
Chambers, William Isaac 19
children 20, 122, 160, *162*, 181, *193*, *198–9*
Clark, Emma 100
Collins, Gemma 45, 93, 172, 178
Córdoba Mosque 26, 49, 70, *71*
Critchlow, Keith 41–58, *42–3*, *46–7*, *58–61*, *174–9*, 181
    designs *13*, 147, *151*, *159*, 160, *161*, 164, *168*
    drawings *10*, *165*

Dean, Nick *187*
dome *13*, 38, *43*, *74*, *108*, *151*, 164, *165–71*, 172, *173*
doors *54–7*, *90–1*, *179*

entrance *14*, *105*, *113–16*, *130–3*
Eşrefoğlu Mosque, Turkey *28*

floor *44*, 129, *134–5*, *139*
fountain *14*, *105*, *106*, *107*, *111*, *113–16*

Gangat, Zakarya 184–5
gardens 100, 104–7, *105–13*, 122
geometric patterns *13*, 41–58, *42–3*, *161*, *168*

Glancey, Jonathan 25
grilles, decorative 147, *174–5*

Hetherington, Alex (guide) 182

idealism, practising 31–8
Ihsan (guide) 122, 128–9, 144, 147, 158–60
Islam, Yusuf (Cat Stevens) 6, 23

King's College Chapel 26, *27*, 29, 49, 93, *94*
Kutlu, Hüseyin 97, 164

Lantern atrium, London *39*
learning space 144, 185, *188–9*
Leitner, Gottlieb 19
light, natural *83*, 89, 144, 147, *154*, 158, *170–1*
lighting 50, *50*, 88
London Eye 25, 33, *33–5*, 37, 38

Maidment, Mark 86, 88
Marks Barfield Architects 24–6, 31–8, 66–9, *94–5*, *102–4*, *166–8*
    Mashrabiya *59*, *159*
    mihrab *161*, *176–8*
    research/plans 17, 29, *48*, 87, *98*, 104
    sustainability principles 85, 87
Marks, David *9*, 24–6, 29, 31–8, 41–2, 45, 70–1, 85, 93, 98, 100, *101*
marquetry *54–7*, 91, 147, *159*, *179*
mashrabiya 21, 50, *59*, *154*, 159–60, *159*, *164*
Medina Mosque, early 17, *26*
Mekic, Sejad 17, 129, 159, 181–2, *184*
mihrab 21, 29, 97, *154*, 158, 160, 164, *176–8*
Miller, Ibn Ali *187*
minbar 29, 49, *154*, 164
Mohammed, Khalil 20
mortuary 185, *196*

Pevsner, Nikolaus 19–20, 21
Portcullis House, London 93
portico 90, *114–79*, 122, *128–9*
prayer hall *61*, *83*, *124–7*, *146–57*, 147, 158–60, 164, *167*, 172, *198*

qibla wall 18, 21, 100, *167*
Rahman, Sayedur 93
Rahman, Shahida 63
residencies, on-site *197*
Ressel, Guilherme 42, 49–50, 58
roof 26, 88, 90, 97, 147, 172
Rudolph, Ian 24–5, 29, 45

Saleem, Shahed 17, 18, 29, 45
Schaffner, Jephtha 71, 74, 76
screens 21, 50, 58, *59*, *154*, 159–60, *159*, *164*
Seal, Helen 104–7
Shah Jahan Mosque, Woking 19–21, *19*
Shrine of Sayyid Ni'matullah Wali, Mahan *70*
Sinan 42, 49
Skelly & Couch 86, 89, 90
stained glass *60*, *155*, 172
suras 70, 97, 122, 128, 160, 164
sustainability 50, 74, 85–91, 122, 144

tiles 144, *144–5*, 164
tree design 26, 50, *51–3*, 63–80, *64–9*, *72–83*, 147
Treetop Walkway, Kew Gardens 31, *32*, 38

Ulugh Beg Madrasa, Samarkand *99*
University of Cambridge Primary School 37, 38

vaulting 26, *27*, 29, 49, *53*, 93, *96*, 97
ventilation *61*, 88, 90, *90*
visitors 182, *186–95*

walls 18, 21, 86, 98, 100, *124–7*, 128, *167*
weddings 144, *191–2*
Westminster Abbey 49, *96*
windows *60*, *124*, *155*, 172
Wingrove, Matthew 85, 90–1
Winter, Tim *9*, 22–5, 45, 48, 80, 158, 160, 164, *187*, *190*, *193*
women's areas 144, *145*, 147, *154*, 160, *161–3*, *176–8*

208 CAMBRIDGE CENTRAL MOSQUE